THE INDIAN CARIBBEAN

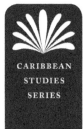

CARIBBEAN
STUDIES
SERIES

ANTON L. ALLAHAR AND NATASHA BARNES
Series Editors

THE INDIAN CARIBBEAN

Migration and Identity in the Diaspora

LOMARSH ROOPNARINE

University Press of Mississippi / Jackson

www.upress.state.ms.us

The University Press of Mississippi is a member of the Association of American University Presses.

Copyright © 2018 by University Press of Mississippi
All rights reserved
Manufactured in the United States of America

First printing 2018

∞

Library of Congress Cataloging-in-Publication Data

Names: Roopnarine, Lomarsh, author.
Title: The Indian Caribbean : migration and identity in the diaspora / Lomarsh Roopnarine.
Description: Jackson : University Press of Mississippi, 2018. | Series: Caribbean studies series | Includes bibliographical references and index. | Identifiers: LCCN 2017029430 (print) | LCCN 2017051725 (ebook) | ISBN 9781496814395 (epub single) | ISBN 9781496814401 (epub institutional) | ISBN 9781496814418 (pdf single) | ISBN 9781496814425 (pdf institutional) | ISBN 9781496814388 (hardcover : alk. paper)
Subjects: LCSH: East Indians—Caribbean Area—History. | East Indians—Caribbean Area—Ethnic identity. | Caribbean Area—Emigration and immigration—History. | India—Emigration and immigration—History. | East Indian diaspora.
Classification: LCC F2191.E27 (ebook) | LCC F2191.E27 R66 2018 (print) | DDC 972.9/004914—dc23
LC record available at https://lccn.loc.gov/2017029430

British Library Cataloging-in-Publication Data available

CONTENTS

Contents

THE INDIAN CARIBBEAN

INTRODUCTION

Perhaps a sound way to start this book is to ask some fundamental questions. Why another book on Indians in the Caribbean? How is this book different from other books? What does this book contribute? What are some new trends that would generate discussions and debates? How will this book move the literature on Indian Caribbean people forward? These questions not only are warranted but also are important because the published studies on Indians in the Caribbean, especially in history and culture, are repetitious. Over the past twenty-five years, myriad books have told very much the same story about Indians in the Caribbean, especially books on the indenture period. The primary reason for the repetitiousness in such books is that researchers have tended to use and rely on archival records rather than applying techniques of oral history to write about the Indian experience in the Caribbean (see Roopnarine 2014a). An examination of this methodological approach to understanding Indian Caribbean people has revealed more reliance on institutions and less on the voices of the people themselves. The voices of the people, whether collected through oral history or ethnography, give participants an opportunity to tell in their own words their versions of their own experiences and events. This approach is critically important because, if not applied, the participants' voices and views of themselves will be distorted and drowned out.

There are also imbalances in the literature on Indian Caribbean people. Much more attention has been paid to their history and culture. Less attention has been paid to issues of migration and identity. Also, more attention has been paid to Guyana, Trinidad, and Suriname (Indophone Caribbean), home to a majority of Indians in the Caribbean. The French Caribbean and other islands with smaller Indian populations have been marginalized in the study of Indian Caribbean people. The story of Indians in these islands with smaller Indian populations is considered minor history. Professor Sudesh

Misra espouses that "minor history is not defined by the absence of momen-
tous events; it is characterized, rather, by the presence of quasi-events, or
events whose eventful status is in dispute, inside the theatre of major history"
(2012). Misra adds that minor histories have remained "half-forgotten in the
lower depths and are deemed to be minor because they have failed the test
of significance inside the major event" (2012). This has certainly been the
case where Indians are a minority in the Caribbean. Their history has often
been placed in the margins of Indian Caribbean historiography. It is time
for this history to be moved from the margins to the mainstream through
discovery and recovery. Events of minor history and society are important
because when they are included in the larger history they can lead to the
discovery of similar minor events, and when these minor events are linked
together they can provide alternative ways to view and voice the history of
people and their institutions.

The published studies on Indians in the Caribbean have also shown an
insular approach, reflecting Indocentric threads and trends. The theory
behind this approach is that the only credible perspectives in the exploration
of Indian history and culture are those of the descendants of Indian people.
This is misleading. The country and ethnocentric approach jeopardizes
the ability to achieve objectivity in the study of Indian Caribbean people.
What is needed is a comparative approach with inclusive themes that cut
across the Indian Caribbean diaspora without losing sight of substantive
and unique themes within each country. Comparative studies of Indians in
the Caribbean are rare. Yet, comparative historical analysis has existed for
some time and has produced significant findings when applied. The lack of
the application of comparative studies has resulted in the bigger questions
about the Indian experience in the Caribbean being missed. For example,
what are some elements that bind or separate Indian Caribbean people? How
have they evolved as a people since indentured emancipation? How have
they been perceived by the wider Caribbean society in their drive toward
human and societal development? What are some challenges they face in
an ever-globalizing world? Unfortunately, the term *Indian diaspora* in the
Caribbean is more symbolic than practical. Indians have little or no contact
with other Indians in the Caribbean, even in the age of globalization. For
instance, Guyanese Indians have little contact with Indians in the French
Caribbean. Also, little attention has been paid to the arrival of nonindentured
Indians in the Caribbean since the 1900s. This migration to the Caribbean
has gone unremarked upon by researchers. In Guyana, Trinidad, and Suriname these recent Indian migrants are practically invisible due to the large

Indian populations in these places, but they are visible in other Caribbean islands with smaller Indian populations. Their ethnicity simply stands out against the mainly African Caribbean population. Who are these recent arrivals? What brought them to the Caribbean? What are they doing in the Caribbean? What is their relationship with former indentured communities and the wider Caribbean?

The pattern of publication on the Caribbean shows an overwhelming focus on the larger ethnic groups, even when Indians make up the majority population in the southern Caribbean countries of Guyana, Trinidad, and Suriname. Indians make up an estimated 12 percent of the population of the English-speaking Caribbean. Yet, the history, culture, and identity of minority groups like Indians have been subsumed under that of the majority population. Migration scholars were too busy studying the unprecedented wave of Caribbean nationals to Europe and North America following the Second World War. They had no practical reason to believe that ethnicity would play a vital role in Caribbean migration studies. They thought that the people of the Caribbean migrated for the same basic reasons. Nonetheless, since the last decade of the twentieth century, ethnicity has become an important and unavoidable factor in Caribbean migration studies. Scholars have now turned their attention to ethnicity and migration, yet the attention on Indians in the Caribbean has lagged behind. This omission is unfortunate because minority groups also experience unique social dynamics, sometimes with greater intensity than majority groups. They are often singled out and subjected to unequal treatment in their new society. Furthermore, in an era of globalization, some minority groups strive to maintain their own identity formation because they do not want to be homogenized or assimilated into a single-world society. Minority groups are also the product of the same global forces that help to shape, develop, and contribute to the Caribbean and other related enclaves.

This book is about Indian Caribbean migration and identity formation and deals particularly with Indians who have evolved through the indenture system from the nineteenth to the twenty-first centuries. These individuals are called People of Indian Origin (PIO), that is, their ancestors were born in India but they are not citizens of India. In recent times, the Indian government has extended the opportunity for PIOs to apply for Indian citizenship. This opportunity is forward looking in terms of India renewing contacts with Caribbean Indians that actually ceased nearly one hundred years ago after indenture emancipation. From a critical point of view, this opportunity might have come too late since Caribbean Indians have evolved into a unique Caribbean population without any continuous meaningful contact with India, at least with the lower classes of Indians. India has little relevance to most Caribbean Indians. They possess very little knowledge of India other than what has been handed down to them by their indentured ancestors. Yet, Caribbean Indians have been shaped by Indian subcontinent customs such as the Hindu religion, music, folklore, and Bollywood films. Caribbean Indians have developed an in-between status. They are not like Indians in India, nor are they like Caribbean Creoles. Instead, they have merged India and the Caribbean to produce a distinct and dynamic local entity. Ethnomusicologist Peter Manuel writes eloquently that while Indians in the Caribbean have experienced "assimilation, creolization, and a degree of cultural rupture . . . many aspects of traditional culture flourished like transplants in the new homeland's fertile soil; in some cases, they change or evolve significantly, but less through acculturation or external influences than through orthogenetic development or consolidation and streamlining of related Old World traditions" (2015, 12).

One chapter of this book focuses on the second wave of East Indian migration to the Caribbean, known technically as non-resident Indians (NRIs). NRIs are individuals who have Indian citizenship but live outside of India. These individuals arrived in the Caribbean without an indentured contract or after indenture emancipation but have remained and formed significant populations or communities in the Caribbean, like those in Barbados, the US Virgin Islands, and Jamaica (see Nakhuda 2013; Mansingh and Mansingh 2000). This contemporary aspect of Indian migration to the Caribbean has escaped scholarly attention and deserves a full book—beyond what is provided in this volume. To date, there isn't a book on Indian migration or Indian identity in the Caribbean. Instead, there are some articles that have examined both themes, but they have focused on the migration from India to the Caribbean during indenture and from the Caribbean to Europe and North America since the Second World War. Much less scholarly attention has been paid to Indian migration within each island and within the Caribbean region. The lack of migration studies on Indian Caribbean people suggests that Indians are habitually nonmigratory. This suggestion is invalid and surprising since Indians are obviously in the Caribbean because of migration and economic incentives. That they would continue this pattern of migration even within constraints would seem logical. Even before Indians were brought to the Caribbean, they were migrating in and out of India mainly for employment and religious reasons. This desire to move continued in the Caribbean despite obstacles. The colonial state implemented restrictive ordinances to contain Indian laborers on specific plantations to ensure surveillance and control. Indian customs also impeded migration because many were simply comfortable with a more secure and supportive rural lifestyle. After indenture emancipation, Indians moved from the plantations to independent settlements, then from settlements to urban areas. Indian Caribbean people have been a meaningful portion of the migratory workers, traders, professionals, and businessmen whose skills and acumen have helped to develop the Caribbean region. This movement and subsequent contributions have been possible because Caribbean Indians have understood the importance of adapting to Western education and culture to achieve upward social mobility. The transformation of their social structure from caste to class is one main factor that has compelled Indians to take up modern standard languages (English, French, or Dutch), education, and jobs. Since the Second World War, Indians have been migrating from their Caribbean base to their colonial former mother country in Europe and North America, creating a second Indian diaspora after the first wave of indentured migrants to the Caribbean. These Indians overseas are products of twice migration, or what journalist Joseph Berger for the *New York Times* (2014) calls "twice removed," with a triple consciousness of India, the Caribbean, and Western developed countries. From their European and North American enclaves, they have created transnational networks linking their departed and new homelands. More recently, Indians have acquired a new visibility across the Caribbean, North America, and Western Europe because of political, economic, and social transformation; liberalization of immigration laws; and globalization.

For the majority of Indian Caribbean people, especially the large working class, migration is really a product of the interplay between constraints and thought, will and eventual action. Migration has always been dictated by occupation, education, income, and religion, which gives the movement across boundaries a distinct and divisive character. Yet, amid aspirations toward modernity, Indians do not necessarily dismiss their preexisting values—education, gender relations, and family cohesion and connection—when they migrate. Migration is also associated with ridicule. In the Caribbean, working-class Indians, especially from Guyana, are not wanted in Barbados and Trinidad because they are seen more as a burden than a benefit. They are not considered immigrants but invaders. They are blamed for an upsurge in crime, pressure on resources, and illegal activities. Therefore, the issue is not that Indians have not migrated but rather under what circumstances and conditions their migration occurred. How have the larger structural

conditions in which they live determined, limited, or even expanded opportunities to migrate? How have they approached and responded to these
opportunities? How have these opportunities modified their own lives as
well as their former and new societies, economies, and governments? In
other words, how has migration changed the living and working conditions
of Indian Caribbean people as well as those of the wider community?

The examination of Indian identity in the Caribbean has also raised concerns. Researcher Thomas Eriksen writes: "Indians in a poly-ethnic society
outside of India cannot adequately be viewed simply as Indians. They are
Indians embedded in a particular historical and socio-cultural context, and
this fact is an inextricable part of their life—even those aspects of their life
which pertain to their very Indianness" (1992). Certainly Indians have more
in common with other ethnic groups in the Caribbean than with Indians in
India or even with non-resident Indians in the Caribbean, mainly because
of a shared plantation experience. However, Indians in the Caribbean have
not evolved as a uniform entity. There are, of course, some shared internal
characteristics, for example, in religion, but they have evolved differently in
different regions of the Caribbean. Yet, for the past two decades, the published
research on Indian identity in the Caribbean has not moved beyond static
assumptions and explanations. The discourse on Indian identity has revolved
around cultural retention (Klass 1961), assimilation (Nevadomsky 1980a,
1980b), creolization (Smith 1965), Coolitude (Carter and Torabully 2002), and
douglarization (Puri 2004). Notwithstanding limitations, these concepts have
added to the understanding of Indian identity in the Caribbean. Nonetheless, alternative analyses are warranted. For the past decade, questions as to
what constitutes an Indian identity in the Caribbean have been the center
of discussions and debates at many major international conferences. Some
specific questions have been asked: How does one define an Indian or what
makes someone an Indian? What does Indo-Caribbean mean? Is the term
Indo-Caribbean only used in the Caribbean diaspora? Can a Muslim Indian
be considered an Indian in the Caribbean? This last question was asked by
Suriname's noted historian Maurits Hassankhan at the Indentured Labor
Route International Conference in Mauritius on November 2–5, 2014. These
questions have raised issues that are an integral part of the global trend. How
do Indians in the Caribbean see themselves in an ever-globalizing world?
Have they retained their ancestral identity? Have they become increasingly
interconnected with other world cultures through the forces and facets of
globalization? Or have they resisted assimilation and instead shown a quest
for a separate identity, be it ethnic, religious, or regional?[1]

This book offers two sets of alternative analyses of Indian identity in the Caribbean. The first is Coolieology, that is, a theoretical as well as a practical framework that argues that Indians in the Caribbean have not overcome the indignities of indenture. The concept of Coolieology espouses that the approach Indians have taken before, during, and after indenture has not eased the pain and suffering they encountered on and beyond the plantations. The first part (Coolie) of the term Coolieology symbolizes pain, while the second part (ology) represents the lingering saga of dealing with pain from the depot to the sea voyage to the plantations to now. Coolieology does not seek to apply a Band-Aid approach to the suffering Indians endured in the Caribbean and indentured Indian diaspora. Instead, it seeks to understand how the evils of indenture have prevented Indians from developing a sound identity. It is a concept that is not static but rather a never-ending process of dealing with suffering and finding a secure place and space that will lessen the uneasiness of Caribbean Indians in relation to themselves first and the wider society, including India, second.

The second alternative analysis of Indian identity is a multipartite approach that argues that Creole identity (Euro-African) does not apply to a majority of Caribbean Indian groups. The identity of Indians in the Caribbean can be conceptualized on an ethno-local, an ethno-national, a trans-Caribbean, and a global level. Ethno-local identity emphasizes how Indians transferred but struggled to maintain their ancestral customs and culture in certain areas in the Caribbean, while ethno-national identity underscores how Indians identify with their nation of birth in specific Caribbean countries but in relation with their ethnicity. Trans-Caribbean identity shows how Indians identify with other Indian Caribbean countries. Global Indian identity demonstrates how globalization and modernization have led to a global or universal Indian identity in the insular Caribbean environment. Within all four sections, there is demonstrated a sense of struggle to maintain these identities. There is some overlap in this multipartite structure of Indian identity. Moreover, the geographical space is not static. For instance, the expression of a national identity does not mean that Indians have to remain in their nation of birth. The central argument of this model is that identity is negotiated and shaped by geography, history, political leadership, migration, and globalization, which is not totally physical or permanent but is also imaginative, incorporating issues of ethnicity, resistance, and human rights, among other factors.

The interplay of migration and identity formation might not have been central to the Caribbean experience and certainly was not central to the imperial migration project. But Indian migration and identity formation did intersect and interact with the overall Caribbean migration process. To Indians, both processes were not marginal. They were instead an opportunity for transplanted people to create their own space within the larger transplanted world. Migration and identity formation represented an interwoven web of connections, collaborations, and conflicts born out of dire need rather than out of creativity. For the most part, Indian migration was intracolonial; that is, the movement was from one colonized region to another, either from one colony to another (from India to Guyana or from Guyana to Trinidad) or from one colony to the mother country (from Suriname to the Netherlands). This pattern of migration still continues but represents, paradoxically, a privileged movement across borders denied to other migrants. For instance, French Caribbean Indians can travel to France, while a visa is required from migrants outside of French territories. To understand what this privilege means is essentially to understand, for example, the challenges contemporary Indian Guyanese (the poorest in the pan-Indian or Indophone Caribbean) face on a daily basis to obtain a visa to the United States. For these and other reasons, the forms and functions of Indian migration are driven independently but are conditioned by government regulations, which reflect a mix of protection and subordination.

METHODOLOGY

This book is based on over twenty-five years of formal and informal ethnographic research in the Caribbean and the North American Indian community. Although I did not collect data formally, I started examining Indian migration when I was in New Nickerie, Suriname, in 1980. There, I witnessed a wave of Indian Guyanese entering Suriname to work in the agricultural and construction sectors of the economy. I was a part of this wave of migrants who immersed themselves in intraregional migration. In the early 1980s, I immigrated to the United States, and from this base I contacted and visited various Indian communities, collecting and recording data on Indian migration. In the 1990s, I visited Guyana and Suriname numerous times, and from this experience I witnessed firsthand how thousands of Indo-Guyanese and Indo-Surinamese were active in migration, some illegally. From 2002 to 2012, I lived in the US Virgin Islands, and from these islands I visited many other islands—including Trinidad, and Antigua— with significant Indian populations due to inward and outward migration. As a result, I have published two articles on Indian Caribbean intraregional migration. Since 2012 I have been living in the United States collecting data on Caribbean Indians in New York, New Jersey, and Toronto through conversations and oral narratives. I have also visited Guyana, Trinidad, and Suriname, again conducting full and semistructured interviews with about one hundred participants. The ages of the participants vary from eighteen to eighty, and the interviewees are of different classes, religions, and genders. Ethnographic models of research are useful for studying the contemporary intra- and extra-regional migration, where information is limited for Indian migration. Conversational narratives add another layer to the whole process of exploring migration and identity formation.

Qualitative and, to some extent, quantitative methods are applied. Archival and secondary sources are used for the historical period of Indian migration. However, these sources are carefully analyzed to arrive at objectivity. Throughout this book, the main approach is to rely less on institutions and more on the voices of migrants and other people, although I am aware that what people say is not always accurate. People, as opposed to institutions, tend to reveal lived experiences normally not found in written sources. The section on Indian identity is highly influenced by debates, discussions, and discourses from Indian diaspora conferences and from scholars in the field of Indian Caribbean studies. From these interactions and conversations, there seems to be an urgent need to develop alternatives modes and models of analyses on Indian identity in the Caribbean. I have introduced Coolieology and the multipartite analysis of Indian identity (ethno-local, ethno-national, trans-Caribbean, and global), drawing upon published studies and ethnographic research.

I have immersed myself in the Indian Caribbean communities and the Indian Caribbean communities abroad and have gained deep knowledge of the inner workings of migration and identity formation, which could not be obtained from second-hand sources. I was very careful not to impose my own views. I was able to gauge what people said they did and what they actually did. I tried, whenever possible, to get into the hearts and minds of participants. Like any other study, there are limitations. Research was not conducted in the French West Indies and in Europe (Britain, France, and the Netherlands), although I did conduct research at the National Archives in Kew Gardens, London, on the historical aspects of Indian migration to the Caribbean. However, e-mail interviews were conducted with prominent scholars who have written on the Indian diaspora, many of them living in the diaspora. Such limitations notwithstanding, I would not have written this book if I were not convinced that a study of Indian migration and identity would contribute to the understanding of Indians in the Caribbean and the diaspora. The intent of the book is to mark and celebrate 2017 as the one-hundred-year anniversary of the abolition of indentured immigration to the Caribbean.

REVIEW OF INDIANS IN THE CARIBBEAN

The purpose here is to provide a general overview of Indians in the Caribbean. Readers interested in learning more about Indians during indenture are referred to my previous book *Indo-Caribbean: Resistance and Accommodation*, and for the modern period, see Viranjini Munasinghe's book, *Callaloo or Tossed Salad?: East Indians and the Cultural Politics of Identity in Trinidad*. Indians began to arrive in the Caribbean soon after the emancipation of African slaves during the latter part of the nineteenth century (in the British Caribbean in 1838; the Danish and French Caribbean in 1863; and the Dutch Caribbean in 1873). The movement of Indians to the Caribbean was one segment of a larger movement to have Indians replace slave labor wherever African slavery was abolished. Indians were shipped to Mauritius, La Reunion, Strait Settlement, Fiji, Natal, South Africa, British Guiana, Trinidad, Suriname, Guadeloupe, Martinique, French Guiana, Jamaica, Belize, St. Lucia, St. Vincent, Grenada, St. Kitts, and St. Croix. For Caribbean Indian population statistics, see table 1 in chapter 1. Indians would have also been shipped to Latin America had not the British government turned down Spain's request to experiment with indentured Indian labor. Spain instead brought Chinese contract laborers to its Latin American colonies. The story of indentured labor and its implications has been well established (see Hoefte 1998; Shepherd 1994; Laurence 1994; Look Lai 1993; Dabydeen and Samaroo 1987). It is commonly accepted that Indians chose to work in the Caribbean mainly because of socioeconomic reasons brought about by their own internal oppressive social system and the impact of British colonialism. These contract workers were mainly rural peasants who were not totally aware of the terms of their contract or the severity of plantation work that awaited them in the Caribbean. Some were duped and kidnapped into indenture, while a majority left their homeland willingly. Whatever might have been their reasons for leaving, they realized quickly that they were going to an unfamiliar place to work for about five years and then return home. The main aspects of their labor contracts were basic, "free" housing; fringe medical care; rights to return passages; fixed daily wages; and continuous employment with one employer. When their contracts expired, they were given an option to re-indenture and receive small parcels of land in lieu of their return passages. Of the estimated five hundred thousand Indians shipped from India during indenture, about two-thirds of them chose to stay in the Caribbean—a majority in Guyana, Trinidad, and Suriname.

As soon as Indians signed indenture contracts in India, they were kept in various depots until the allotted number was reached to ship them to the Caribbean. The depot quickly developed a reputation for being a world of its own, comprising Indians from various caste and religious backgrounds, speaking different dialects as well as displaying different behavioral traits. This experience was extended to the three-to-four-months-long sea journey to the Caribbean, although married and single women were placed in separate quarters onboard the ships. Over time, Indians began to view the sea voyage with trepidation, especially around the southern tip of Africa, which they called *Pagla Samoondar* (Mad Sea). In a conversation with the prominent Trinidadian scholar Brinsley Samaroo, I realized that the most dangerous part of the sea journey from India to the Caribbean was around the southern tip of Africa. The waves were notorious. But interestingly, a number of babies were born during the sea voyage, and hence, a child born at sea was named *Samoondar* (male) or *Samoondari* (female), which means born at sea. This information might be useful to contemporary Indians who wish to trace their roots. Their sea voyage experience was simply dreadful: disease, death, rape, anxiety, and fear were common. The journey was like living in a floating prison and was a grim introduction to the plantation experience in the Caribbean.

In the Caribbean, the indentured Indians were dispatched in groups of thirty to forty people to various plantations, occupying barracks that African slaves had recently vacated. The plantations were like *Nakra* (Hell) or prisons without walls. They were governed by a series of elaborate labor ordinances that effectively put the power in the hands of the planters. Indians were subjected to strict labor laws and long hours of arduous work, they were flogged, and, above all, they had to carry a pass. Failure to carry out their duties was met with the harshest punishment, fines, and imprisonment. The entire indenture system was characterized by injustices, particularly toward Indian women. The imbalanced male-to-female ratio of one hundred to twenty-five placed women at a major disadvantage in their homes on the plantations. They were exposed to abuse and experienced rape and murder by their own Indian counterparts as well as from the planter class (see Mohapatra 1995). Despite the authoritarian structure of the plantation system, Indians continued to come to the Caribbean, averaging about three thousand to four thousand per year in some colonies. Their presence helped to revolutionize the sugar plantation system.

In the plantation environment of "survival of the fittest," Indians came to rely on their own cultural resilience for survival, especially *ganw-ke-rishta* (village relations). On their journey to the Caribbean, they formed close social ties of *Dipwa-Bhai* and *Dipwa-Bahin* (depot brothers and sisters) and *Jahaja Bhai* and *Jahaja Bahin* (ship brothers and sisters) across caste and religion and created a semblance of lost India through religious observances, festivals, and feasts. They were able to maintain the main aspects of their religions, especially Hindu and Islam. Their caste system, however, broke down in the face of pressure from a Western-oriented plantation system that did not recognize caste principles. Actually, the caste system in the Caribbean has become extinct as descendants of indentured Indians were increasingly less exposed to it. The door on this aspect of Indian ethnicity is effectively closed, and there have been no significant attempts to revive or reconstruct a caste system in the Caribbean. By the 1900s, the indenture system had become unpopular, mainly because of the exploitation of planters and continuous pressure and criticism in India, Britain, and the Caribbean that resulted in, first, the stoppage of any further influx of indentured migrants in 1917 and then the abolition of the indenture system in 1920.

POSTINDENTURE EXPERIENCE

One of the positive aspects of the indenture system was that the Indian indenture experience inadvertently prepared the Indians to deal with the reality of plantation life and beyond. The planters' rigorous labor regimen and routine as well as the laborers' adaptation and adjustment to this process led to an experienced and dynamic peasant class of Indians. During indenture, Indians learned how to cultivate sugarcane, rice, cocoa, and other crops. After indenture, they used their savings to buy vacant land and utilized their agricultural skills to cultivate the aforementioned crops and raise cattle. By the 1940s, Indians had made an indelible mark on the agriculture sector in some Caribbean colonies. From their agricultural base, they did not only expand their farming activities but also began to penetrate the economic and political spheres of many Caribbean colonies. Yet, they did not totally give up their ancestral customs, although they did make necessary adjustments to their new Westernized homeland. Postindenture Indians were combining their old traditional ways with new ones. Moreover, as Indians began to settle in their new environment, as their population grew, and as the gender imbalance began to equalize, the reliance on spiritualism (Hindu and Islam) as a means of survival gradually gave way to economic materialism. Subsequently, this new focus on material well-being in the lives of Indians inspired them to stake claims beyond their broad agricultural base.

However, it would be a mistake to suggest that their experiences were uniform. In colonies such as St. Lucia, Grenada, St. Vincent, and Jamaica, for example, where Indians were a numerical minority, they were practically absorbed and assimilated into the Creole society. Their small population size, the role of Christian missionaries, interethnic marriages, and the exposure to Western education and employment opportunities sped up the process of Indian cultural assimilation to the Creole society. Nonetheless, Indians in these Caribbean colonies have maintained ethnic residential separation but have submitted to Creole norms and values. In these hybrid communities, everything that was Indian essentially declined as the Indian population lost touch with India or the Indian Caribbean diaspora, although some Indians within these communities do recognize and celebrate significant Indian events and holidays. To sum up, where Indians are a minority or at least less than 5 percent of the population in the Caribbean, they have not made a mark on those islands other than existing in a position of marginality. They have lost all individuality relating to India or to the Indian Caribbean diaspora, except for traces of Hindu and South Indian religion. They have now experienced several generations of ethnic intermarriages and have little significant memory of their immigrant origins. There have not been any concerted efforts from the majority-population Caribbean Indian nations nor from India to provide any significant influence to restore or reconstruct any sense of Indianness for these minorities. These small-population transplants have migrated to other countries outside of the Caribbean or have remained in their rural base. This has been noticeable in the French Caribbean islands of Martinique and Guadeloupe, where an estimated sixty-eight thousand Indians were brought to labor on sugar plantations (see table 1 in chapter 1). Martinique received South Indians (Madrases), while Guadeloupe received North Indians (Kalkatiyas). In Martinique, Indians are still peasants engaging in small-scale sugar production with little ancestral cultural affiliation. But in Guadeloupe, they have preserved some Indian customs and have integrated into the wider society. Nonetheless, their cultural retention and efforts to reconstruct their homeland were severely affected by a French colonial policy of forced assimilation to French values (see Northrup 2000).

In contrast, where Indians enjoy a majority population (Guyana, Trinidad, and Suriname), their postindenture experience has shown qualities of dynamism and depth through land ownership; cultural persistence; cultural assimilation and political participation; business engagement; access to education (medicine and law); and strong connections with India. Indians are well integrated in these countries. Indians have progressed remarkably well economically. This is perhaps not surprising since it was primarily economic incentives that drove them to indenture themselves to the Caribbean. Through hard work, thrifty habits, and investment, Indians have been able to dominate the agricultural and business sectors of these countries. In Berbice, Guyana, and New Nickerie, Suriname, Indians practically own the rice industry, while in Trinidad they have become an economic force in trade, commerce, and business. Indians also have made significant strides in maintaining and developing their institutional culture, which sprung primarily from resistance to European and African norms and values. The loss of and lust for ancestral homeland as well as their deep desire for literacy and learning propelled them to reconstruct and re-create their customs whenever possible. There is a general sense of cultural awareness, assertiveness, and pride based on Hinduism, Islam, Indian weddings, music, dance, festivals, and religious and cultural centers across Guyana, Trinidad, and Suriname. Obviously, not all things Indian survived in the new homeland. The most noticeable omissions are caste and language. Caste disappeared because of the Westernization of the plantations, and except for Sarnami or Hindustani in Suriname and marginal Bhojpuri in Trinidad, which are "plantation-derived Hindi," all transplanted Indian languages are practically gone. There has been little attempt to revive them, particularly in Guyana, even at a museum level. Finally, an estimated 40 percent of Indians in the Caribbean live below the poverty level, and the figure is much higher in Guyana—probably over 50 percent. Taken together, these Indian communities have experienced high rates of suicide, mass migration, domestic abuse, and wealth disparity. They rely heavily on remittances, especially in Guyana and Suriname, from Indians in the North American and European diaspora. Externally, Indians and Africans continue to be at odds with each other based on racial and ethnic tensions as well as the competition for political power.

THE FOCUS OF THE BOOK

Chapter 1 examines the reasons and circumstances in India and the Caribbean that led to the arrival of Indians to the Caribbean plantations. The argument is that the movement of Indians to the Caribbean was not based merely on push factors in India and pull factors in the Caribbean, as explained in previous studies. Rather, the movement of Indians to the Caribbean has more to do with the expansion of world capitalism and the program of imperialism and colonialism. Internal or domestic causes in India as well as in the Caribbean were instigated by the superstructure of the more powerful capitalist movement.

Chapter 2 argues that Indians were brought to the Caribbean under a series of restrictive colonial policies that stymied free movement. Nonetheless, it is argued that some Indians challenged these policies in innovative ways to exercise their rights to migrate. Some took illegal actions and deserted the plantations, while others waited until their contracts expired to migrate. The number of Indians who migrated was smaller than those who remained in their residencies, but migration was a permanent feature of the plantation system that lasted as long as the period of indenture.

Chapter 3 shows that the planters' policies of land acceptance in lieu of return passages and the violation of the return passage contract did not deter an estimated one-third of indentured Indians from returning to their homeland. The process of returning home was frustrating, but returnees used the Immigration Department to exercise their right to return. Not all Indians returned home empty handed. Some returned with significant savings. However, upon their return they were subjected to a host of community caste customs that essentially used up their savings in order to reinstate them into their former social status. Others did not go back to villages but settled in urban areas or migrated back to the Caribbean for a second time. Some arrived in the Caribbean after serving indenture in other colonies like in Mauritius, Fiji, Natal, and so forth.

Chapter 4 analyzes the migration of Indians from their rural plantation base to urban areas and from these areas to other Caribbean countries. This movement has much to do with opportunities in urban areas and some destinations in the Caribbean, as well as the aspirations and motivations of Indians themselves to migrate. In these new places, Indians competed for scarce resources, and as a consequence, they faced bouts of stigmatization and discrimination. Nevertheless, Indian migration to these places continues into today because these places have proven to be a safety valve for Indians in terms of job opportunities and better medical and social services. However, Indian migratory behavior represents agents of a brain exchange rather than a brain drain as they continue to develop their host societies and their departed homeland through services, remittances, and other means.

Chapter 5 examines the migration of Caribbean Indians to developed countries in Europe (former mother countries) and North America from the Second World War to today. The chapter shows that special colonial associations with Caribbean countries and Europe as well as political turbulence and economic stagnation have caused Indians to engage in extra-regional migration. However, the change of immigration laws in Britain in particular and in the United States in the early 1960s shifted Indian migration to the latter destination. Of all the migration patterns, extra-regional migration has had the most profound impact on Indian society and culture in the Caribbean. This migration has helped to sustain Indian families and communities in the Caribbean through remittances. In contrast, it has also created unintended consequences in communities in terms of the breakdown of family unity and cohesion. Family members, especially fathers, have been separated for long periods because of extra-regional migration. The chapter also examines the return migration of Indians to the Caribbean.

Chapter 6 examines the second wave of Indians to the Caribbean since the early twentieth century. These Indians arrived in the Caribbean on their own volition. Although they make up a significant population and have meaningful connections with the Indian diplomatic community in Guyana, Trinidad, and Suriname, they are not visible in these countries because they tend to blend with the majority Indian population. They are very noticeable in the predominantly African Caribbean islands. The chapter traces the arrival of these recent migrants and assesses what they are doing in the Caribbean as well as their relationships with descendants of indentured Indians and the wider Caribbean ethnic community.

Chapter 7 shows how the phases of migration from indenture to now have shaped Indian identity in the Caribbean. The chapter presents the argument that Indian identity cannot be solely explained by using the creolization model. Rather, it can be conceptualized through Coolieology and the multipartite structure of ethno-local, ethno-national, trans-Caribbean, and global. This chapter argues that Indians have yet to overcome the social ills of indenture and that the multipartite structure approach is convincing because Indian identity has been shaped by geography, history, migration, leadership, technology, and globalization. The final chapter summarizes the findings of this study.

Finally, a note on the term Indian is warranted. The use of the terms Indians and Indian Caribbeans in this book should not be taken to mean Amerindians, the first inhabitants of the region, who are also sometimes referred to in Caribbean history as Indians. The term Indian in this context means individuals who were brought from India to the Caribbean to labor as indentured servants as well as Indians who arrived in the Caribbean since the Second World War. Initially, these immigrants were called East Indians, as they were in India, but after they settled and became more participatory citizens in the Caribbean, most scholars and laypersons began referring to them as Indians, dropping the East from East Indians. Therefore, Caribbean Indians, or Caribbeans of Indian descent whether in the Caribbean or in the overseas diaspora, are referred to as Indians in this study.

Chapter One

THE MIGRATION OF INDENTURED INDIANS FROM INDIA TO THE CARIBBEAN

The previous section provided an introduction to Indian migration and identity. This chapter examines the movement of Indians from their homeland to various Caribbean colonies. The focus is on the circumstances that led to the arrival of Indians in the Caribbean as well as the factors that made them leave their homeland to work in a distant and unfamiliar environment. Particular attention will be paid to the entire organization of the indenture emigration system, recruitment of Indians in India, and their subsequent experience on the long sea voyage from India to the Caribbean. Statistics will be provided on the number, gender, caste, and religion of Indian emigrants to show the magnitude and diversity of the indenture emigration scheme.

QUESTIONS ON INDENTURED EMIGRATION

The majority of original correspondence or archival records on indenture tends to support the view of the planter class that indentured Indians left their homeland because of the push-pull model of migration; that is, people are pushed out of the sending environment because of deprivation and disadvantaged conditions and pulled to the receiving destination because of opportunities for a better livelihood. This explanation would imply that more Indians would have migrated to the Caribbean, since India was considered a poor colony where millions of Indians lived in hapless conditions. However, only five hundred thousand (0.16 percent) Indian citizens migrated to the Caribbean out of a population of over three hundred million. Why did a large proportion of India's population not migrate? Was it because they did not want to? Or was it because their family ties, jobs, culture, and familiar environment made them feel at home? Or could it be that many more had wanted to migrate but were prevented from migrating because of their own poverty and cultural institutional barriers (caste) that isolated them? Were they simply unaware of indenture emigration? Or did the Caribbean plantations have inadequate accommodation to take in more indentured laborers? Did the planters operate simply on demand rather than on the need for a large surplus of labor? It is therefore crucial that the various aspects of Indian indentured emigration be sorted out before any analyses can be made.

First, Indians were involved in migration before they were brought to the Caribbean. Indian indenture emigration to the Caribbean was a form of migration that was in tandem with other world migration patterns in the mid-nineteenth and twentieth centuries. Like other forms of world migration, Indian migration was built on historical instincts to move, although the specificities were different from other world movements. By the nineteenth century, satisfaction with the once settled, stable, and static way of life in a particular environment gave way to the urge to move. In this regard, Indian migration coincided with the age of migration; that is, people were essentially always on the move. Indians were migrating from rural to urban areas as well as to areas around India looking for seasonal and permanent employment. To be sure, only a small percentage of Indians were involved in indenture emigration. But how they have impacted their new environment is more significant than what would seem to be reflected by their small number. Second, indentured emigration was multifaceted, revealing patterns and practices of regular and irregular, temporary and permanent, and manipulative and voluntary trends. Third, indentured Indians were not from a common background. Sure enough, they were mostly peasants and shared a fundamental indentured status, but they were as diverse as India itself. Moreover, the migrants during the first two decades of indenture were remarkably different from those who left India from the 1870s onward. Fourth, no single theory is sufficient to explain any form of migration. Indenture emigration, however, can be explained by applying the historical-structural perspective, or world system model of migration, followed by the push-pull factors of migration. The world system model is a Marxist approach to migration and argues that migration is caused by uneven socioeconomic global capitalist development (Wallerstein 1974; Wood 1982). The theory is that the forces of capitalism penetrate into underdeveloped regions or colonies of the world and distort social and economic relations, which in turn pushes people in these regions to move. Migration is a natural outgrowth of disruptions and dislocations as well as the structure of the world market system in the process of capitalist accumulation and development. In other words, development in the core simply means underdevelopment in the periphery. The main thought in the historical-structural perspective is that when the capitalist economy grows outward from the core into peripheral regions, migration flows are inevitable because the forces of the capitalist economy provide job opportunities in the core, but they also interfere with material bases of survival (land, labor, wages, jobs, culture, etc.) in peripheral regions. However, internal push factors in the periphery are a consequence of the more powerful external capitalist development structure. Over time, the internal push factors will become so structurally embedded in the periphery that external factors may appear invisible. Nonetheless, and in the case of indenture migration, neither the Caribbean nor India was in the developed or underdeveloped world, respectively. Both places were colonies of the British Empire (except the Dutch and French West Indies) and were treated as such, although for different purposes. The British used the Caribbean mainly for the exploitation of sugar, while India was exploited for cotton. In the constant drive for capital accumulation within the British Empire, inadvertent outcomes emerged, such as the creation of a shortage of labor in one area (the Caribbean) because of slave emancipation and a labor surplus in another (India) because of the internal displacement of the peasantry. The colonial planter class believed that these unexpected outcomes could be beneficial to them if they were channeled wisely from one area of the world to another. For the capitalist class, indentured labor was mobile labor. It is within this context that indentured migration occurred (see Roopnarine 2003).

REASONS FOR INDENTURED MIGRATION: FROM THE CARIBBEAN

Indentured Indians were brought to the Caribbean precisely to supplement rather than substitute the lost slave labor on the sugar plantations. The question of whether or not their arrival was a necessary response to the mass exodus of former slaves from the plantations is an analysis for elsewhere. Long before emancipation, the planters had made up their minds to look for an alternative source of labor because they thought the newly freed slaves would reject or withdraw erratically from labor conditions or even revolt against the planters for injustices inflicted on them as slaves. The planters were also searching for a cheap source of labor that they could import with relative ease to use against and control the newly freed slaves' bargaining power for better wages and other plantation amenities. The continuous influx of indentured Indians was also based on failed experiments with other early postemancipation emigration schemes from Africa, the United States, Europe, Madeira, China, and within the Caribbean islands. These emigration experiments failed in terms of steadily supplying labor to the plantations for reasons related to maladjustment, alcoholism, low wages, poor working conditions, tropical heat, and diseases. By contrast, indentured Indians proved to be reliable laborers.

The eventual reliance on indentured Indian laborers to supplement slave labor did not begin in the Caribbean but in Mauritius. The experiment with indentured Indians in this island in the Indian Ocean caught the attention of private sugar planters in the Caribbean, such as British Guianese planter John Gladstone. In a series of letters to the private recruitment firms Messrs Gillanders, Arbuthnot & Company, Gladstone requested and requisitioned for one hundred Indians from India to work on his plantations in British Guiana. He expressed preference for the Dhangers (the tribal hill people), the very type of indentured Indians who were contracted in Mauritius, to serve his plantation. After some negotiations, Gladstone's request for indentured Indians was accepted (see British Parliamentary Papers 1837–38a, 1837–38b).

The first experiment with 396 indentured Indians in British Guiana was a disaster (see Scoble 1840). More than a third of them perished from abuse and poor working and living conditions. The British government suspended indenture emigration to British Guiana the same year it started (1838) and stated that emigration would resume only when the defects in the system were remedied. The government stopped the private importation of indentured laborers and instead placed all responsibilities under state control and under a series of strict regulations. The British crown and Indian governments emphasized a sound recruitment process, a safe and secure transportation system, and a nonabusive plantation experience. They also insisted that a British agent or a British consular as well as a protector should be stationed at the ports of departure in India and on the Caribbean plantation colonies. Finally, the British and Indian governments reserved the right to suspend and stop indenture emigration to the Caribbean colonies if so needed at any time (British Parliamentary Papers 1874, 29–32). The new state guidelines governing the entire indenture system meant the planters were required to negotiate directly with the British crown and Indian government mainly to avoid abuse and to ensure that indentured Indians would be fairly protected outside the crown's jurisdiction.

In 1845, indenture emigration resumed, but it was suspended in 1848 due to financial difficulties. It resumed again in 1851 and was eventually abolished in 1917. From the 1860s, the British and Indian governments were comfortable with the movement of indentured Indians from India to the Caribbean. Colonial governments in St. Lucia, St. Vincent, Grenada, Jamaica, and St. Kitts—all British Caribbean colonies—were permitted to import indentured laborers. This permission did not go unnoticed by other European governments. The French, Dutch, and Danish governments also saw indentured Indians as a possible solution to alleviate the acute labor shortage in their former slave colonies. During a number of independent conventions and negotiations among the French, Danish, and Dutch governments with the British government following 1860, the British government allowed for the importation of indentured Indians to foreign colonies. These foreign governments who wished to participate in the movement of indentured Indians from India had to comply with a series of regulations designed mainly to safeguard against the ill treatment of indentured Indians.

REASONS FOR INDENTURE MIGRATION: FROM INDIA

A majority of indentured Indians who were taken to the Caribbean did not choose to emigrate willingly, particularly during the first half of the indentureship period (1838–80). A number of them were duped into signing contracts while others felt obligated to go to the Caribbean because they had "eaten their recruiters' salt," meaning that their recruiters had invested in them through feeding, clothing, and housing (British Parliamentary Papers 1910b, 30). Stories abound whereby recruiters would supply the basic needs of intending indentured Indians, such as money, clothing, and food, with the intent of trapping them in debt peonage (see Tinker 1974, 123–26). Indentured Indians' main objection to migration, however, was caste inhibition and obligations. To nineteenth-century Indians, including the peasantry, crossing the *kala pani*, or "black water," was an act to avoid until death. The moment an Indian crossed the *kala pani,* his or her caste was gone and could be reinstated only through excruciating and expensive purification ceremonies. Given the strict caste structure of their close-knit villages, few Indians would have risked caste defilement and ostracism for the unknown Caribbean islands. George Grierson (1883), a colonial official, observed that the main objection of Indians to emigration from their villages was caste restrictions, superstition, and religious beliefs. Around the major recruiting centers in India, stories circulated that Indians were taken away to have *mimiai ka tel* (the oil extracted from a Coolie's head by hanging him upside down). British historian Hugh Tinker (1974) espoused that intending indentured Indians were under the assumption that in the Caribbean they would be converted to Christianity, forced to eat beef and pork, and dispossessed of their holy threads. These Indians were also naturally reluctant to travel to the Caribbean. They would rather have worked in their own familiar environment than venture out to some unknown destination. Agricultural job opportunities existed in India itself, especially in tea gardens and in nearby Assam, Burma, and Mauritius. Grierson noticed that the Assam recruiter could easily outbid the Caribbean recruiter because there was no sea to cross, the distance was shorter, and the pay was better.

The aforementioned factors did not stymie all Indians from indenture emigration. The establishment of British colonialism in India was a divisive factor in the movement of Indians from their homeland to overseas indentured communities. British colonialism transformed the relationship between traditional Indian agriculture and handicraft industries. One critic wrote:

> The demand of the industrial revolution generated an imperial policy and made India productive by transforming it from a producer of manufactured goods to a supplier of raw material (mainly cotton) to the British industrial complex. Subsequently, the East Indian social economy and village community systems were altered and a cash economy was introduced. The ultimate result of British policies in India was that new traders, moneylenders, rent rackers and taxation exacted an enormous toll on the natives. Not only were the natives oblivious to these new developments around them, but vast numbers of them were deceived and became indebted in the process. (Roopnarine 2007, 17)

British colonialism was supported through a land revenue system in Bengal known as *zamindari* in Bombay and *ryotwari* in Madras. Under this system, the British used the *zamindars* (lower echelons of the Indian ruling class) to collect revenues and taxes from the natives, which the latter could not afford. The result was that many natives sold their land to meet their financial burden while others desperately sought new ways of linking life with social and economic justice through migration. Thousands of Indians dealt with their economic hardships by drifting to urban and overseas enclaves looking for employment. These displaced individuals were quite willing to migrate overseas to avoid domestic hardships.

There were myriad other reasons why Indians left their homeland to work overseas. Some Indians migrated because of domestic problems, oppressive personal relationships, and family disputes. Some were even running away from the law. Other Indians migrated because of adventure, like the dancing girls who arrived in Suriname in the 1870s. Some Indians were tied to their landlords like slaves and sought any opportunity to escape their socioeconomic bondage. Natural disasters such as floods and famines added to the pool of migrants in the Caribbean. Civil wars, like the Great Sepoy Mutiny of 1857–58, were another cause for migration. Arguably, some of the above reasons for migrating were domestically derived and driven. But external influence and impact cannot be easily dismissed. Take, for example, the impact of natural disasters. The British colonial system did not create natural disasters, but it certainly did not provide the mechanisms to deal with them. The focus was overwhelmingly on extracting as much revenue as possible rather than providing for the basic needs of protection and survival. When disaster struck, the already desperate situation became even more desperate, forcing thousands to flee to safer grounds, including, perhaps, a trip to the Caribbean to become an indentured laborer. Similarly, British superiority and the lack of respect for Indian religious customs caused the Sepoy Mutiny of 1857–58 in India. The natives' revolt against British colonialism had an enormous impact on India. Thousands of Indians fled their homes in the face of destruction and terror. In 1858, 45,838 Indians migrated out of India. Some migrated to the Caribbean simply to avoid arrest and deportation to the convict settlement of Port Blair (see Laurence 1994). In the final analysis, the demands of the British imperial economy caused socioeconomic upheavals in India and subsequently promoted indenture migration on an unprecedented scale. Internal factors were, however, exacerbated and controlled by the superstructure of the more powerful capitalist development. Whatever might have been the reasons that propelled Indians toward indenture, one factor was constant: there was never a shortage of Indians going to the Caribbean. By the 1870s, the Caribbean planters had become selective in choosing what types of Indians they wanted on their plantations, demonstrating that they did not only have a command over labor but a surplus at their disposal. Table 1 shows the number of Indians brought to the Caribbean during indenture. Missing from this table are those Indians who were rejected for being too unfit or unreliable to emigrate and perform plantation work. In 1900, for example, of 15,465 Indian emigrants registered for indenture, 3,089, or 19.97 percent, were rejected, and of this figure, 932, or 6.02 percent, were rejected on account of physical or mental infirmity (see the 1900 *Report on Emigration from the Port of Calcutta to British and Foreign Colonies*). A decade later, the situation had hardly changed. In 1911,

TABLE 1: DESTINATION OF INDIANS INDENTURED IN THE CARIBBEAN		
Destination	No. Indians indentured	Time frame
British Guiana	239,960	1838–1917
Trinidad	143,939	1845–1917
Suriname	43,404	1873–1916
Guadeloupe	42,236	1854–1895
Jamaica	37,027	1845–1914
Martinique	25,404	1854–1899
French Guiana	8,500	1862–1885
Grenada	3,200	1857–1885
Belize	3,000	1880–1917
St. Vincent	2,472	1861–1880
St. Lucia	2,300	1858–1895
St. Kitts	361	1860–1861
Nevis	342	1873–1874
St. Croix	325	1863–1868
Total	551,470	

Source: These figures were compiled from a number of sources. See appendix 1 and 2 in Lomarsh Roopnarine, *Indo-Caribbean Indenture: Resistance and Accommodation* (Kingston, Jamaica: University of the West Indies Press, 2007), 122–25.

of 12,756 Indians waiting in the depots to be shipped to overseas indenture colonies, 1,152 were rejected (see the 1911 *Report on Emigration from the Port of Calcutta to British and Foreign Colonies*). Every year from the 1860s, at least eight hundred Indians were rejected from emigrating while another one hundred deserted the depots and an estimated two hundred changed their minds just before departure. Using these conservative statistics, an estimated sixty thousand to seventy-five thousand Indians probably would have declared their intentions to indenture themselves overseas during the eighty-year period of indenture. But they were either rejected, released owing to their unwillingness to emigrate, or were claimed by their relatives.

The movement of Indians during the aforementioned time period was not fluid. There were a series of commencements, stoppages, and resumptions during the time period for each country (Roopnarine 2007, 124). The figures might not all be accurate, which I have addressed in another article, "A Critique of East Indian Indentured Historiography in the Caribbean" (Roopnarine 2014a). The major problem is to determine who compiled these figures and when. Nonetheless, the figures are important in providing an idea of the size of Indian indenture emigration to the Caribbean. What is new to the emigration statistics is only the shipload of Indians who were brought to Nevis. This is not an error. In 2013, I presented a paper on Indian indenture in the Danish West Indies at the Whim Museum on St. Croix, and a few individuals in the question-and-answer period claimed that their ancestors were brought from India to Nevis (Roopnarine 2014b). The Belize case is unusual. Indians went there in two waves: first from India directly to Belize and then from India to Jamaica and then to Belize. Most Indians were plantation indentures, but those that were taken to French Guiana worked in the gold fields or places deep in the interior region. The death rate among the French Guiana indentures was the highest.

THE ORGANIZATION AND RECRUITMENT OF INDENTURED LABORERS

Caribbean historian Walton Look Lai writes that "indenture experiment embodied many unique features that distinguished it, not only from earlier forms of unfree labour in the region, but even from many other indentured labour experiments taking place simultaneously during the period in other parts of the world, and even in the Americas" (1993, 51). What makes the indenture emigration so unique? The system involved a hierarchy of agencies and officials with duplicating and overlapping responsibilities. Indenture emigration operated in collaboration with the British government, the colonized Indian government, and the colonial government in the colonies. The British government was the most powerful institution in this three-way collaboration. The Dutch, French, and Danish governments were added after the 1860s into the rank of the British government. However, these governments were not only less powerful but were also subject to the indenture immigration rules and regulations established by the British government. The British government could suspend and stop indenture migration immediately in any of the colonies, if so needed. Below these imperial governments were the colonized Indian government and the colonial governments in the Caribbean. The colonized Indian government was genuinely interested in how the indenture system was conducted and at times spoke passionately against injustices and ill treatment of its citizens abroad; but in reality, it was powerless. That is why on many occasions the Indian government stated that it did not want to get mixed up in bargains between the British government and colonial government on pressing indenture issues. The Indian government took a neutral position on indenture whenever it saw fit. The colonial government in the Caribbean actually governed the plantation life of indentured Indians but was largely influenced by the planter class, who had enormous power.

The indenture emigration system functioned in the following way. The government of India appointed protectors of emigration in most regions and districts to monitor the recruitment of Indians. Local judges supervised the judicial aspects of recruitment to ensure that intending indentured Indians understood the terms of their contracts. Medical examinations were conducted to ensure fitness for the long sea journey and plantation work. The respective Caribbean colonial government appointed emigration agents who then employed provincial and district subagents and licensed recruiters. In the Caribbean, each colonial government had an Immigration Department headed by a chief officer (called different names, Protector of Immigrants, Agent-General of Immigrants, or Immigrant Agent-General). The chief immigration officer was assisted by other subimmigration officers, such as inspectors, clerks, and interpreters. The Immigration Department was responsible for the distribution of Indians and the functioning of the indenture system. The distribution of Indian emigrants was determined prior to their arrival through an application specifying the number of emigrants required by the planters. The chief immigration officer and his associates had the right at any time to enter upon any plantation on which indentured Indians were employed and inspect the condition and treatment of emigrants. Finally, the entire indenture system was governed by a series of ordinances.

The first batch of Indians was recruited from Chota Nagpur, the present-day Indian states of West Bengal, Bihar, and Orissa. These recruits were non-Hindu aboriginal tribal people collectively known as "Hill Coolies," or Jangalis. The recruitment of these hill people for labor in the Caribbean was neither substantial nor successful. They preferred to work on the indigo and tea gardens in and around India. They were also ill treated and experienced high death rates in the Caribbean. From the 1860s, recruits were drawn from Bihar and Bengal, the North-West Provinces (currently known as Uttar Pradesh), Oudh, Fyzabad, Gonda, and Basti in the United Province. In 1900, for example, 18,489 Indians were recruited to work overseas, mainly in Mauritius, Fiji, and the Caribbean. Of this number, 2.36 percent came from Bengal; 9.03 percent from Bihar; 54.93 percent from the Northwest Province; 26.34 percent from Oudh; and 7.35 percent from Punjab (see the 1900 *Report on Emigration from the Port of Calcutta to British and Foreign Colonies*). The recruitment of Indians also occurred in South India among the Madras population. While these emigrants were perceived to have done well on the treacherous sea voyage, they simply disliked plantation work. They often resisted plantation work through desertion or engaged in rum drinking until publicly intoxicated. Madras emigrants turned out to be a supplementary source to the whole indenture emigration scheme, constituting a mere 10 percent of all indentured laborers. A smaller number of emigrants were also recruited from the province of Punjab. Like Madras emigrants, the large-scale recruitment of Punjabi emigrants was not encouraged because they were thought to be more militant toward their plantation bosses. Except for unforeseen circumstances in India, such as natural disasters and civil unrest, this pattern of indenture emigration continued more or less until 1917.

On paper at least, the organization of indenture emigration looked sound. In practice, there were weaknesses. While it is difficult to separate how many Indians went willingly and how many involuntarily, unknown numbers were certainly duped and kidnapped into indenture. How many of them were victims of fraudulent recruitment practices is a question of speculation since the statistics on fraudulent practices were never recorded. Tinker claims that there were three responses from the intending indentured Indians with regard to how much they knew about their destinations: (1) some would ask intelligent questions about the conditions; (2) some would not ask questions but listened instead; and (3) some would regard questions with indifference (1974, 120). Surinamese historian Maurits Hassankhan (2011) thinks stories of the recruitment experience from indentured Indians in the Caribbean might be believable but that some are questionable since they might have derived from emotional feelings of missing home and maladjustment to the plantation labor regime. It is safe to say that not more than 10–15 percent of Indians were taken to the Caribbean on fraudulent grounds. What is more accurate is that a majority of Indians did not know what awaited them in the Caribbean, at least during the first two decades of indenture. In the latter stages of the indenture system, Indians had more knowledge of the Caribbean islands because of information filtered back into their villages from time-expired indentured Indians who had returned. Even then, deceitful and romantic methods of recruitment were not altogether eliminated. When resident-based recruiters failed to convince Indians to indenture overseas, newly returned and time-expired indentured Indians from the Caribbean, turned recruiters, were used. These recruiters knew the inner workings of indenture and skillfully used their experience to inveigle intending indentured Indians. The common method was to present a fancy story of easy work, quick money, and religious connection and customs of India in the Caribbean. For instance, recruiters told the intending Indians that they were going to *Sri-Ram* instead of Suriname. To Indians, *Ram* indicates a religious place that sounds like the Ramayana, a Hindu religious text that exemplifies good over evil, duty over self-indulgence, and generosity over selfishness. Likewise, Indians were told they were going to "Chinidad," which means "land of sugar." Chinidad, of course, sounds like China, the country that borders India, thus misrepresenting the long journey they had to endure to the Caribbean. Conversely, the indentured Indians had their own way of defining, discussing, and imagining their new destinations. The islands overseas were called *Tapu*. To the North Indians, Mauritius was known as *Mirich* or *Mirich Desh*. To the South Indians, British Guiana, Demerara, was known as *Damra, Damaraila*, or *Doomra*; Trinidad was known as *Chinitat* (Tinker 1974, 120). Fiji was known as *pheegee*; Burbon as *Birboon*; Natal as *Naatal*; Suriname as *Sriram*. Of all these places, Trinidad was the favorite, and Mauritius was the worst because of the land availability and planters' exploitation, respectively.

The British and Indian governments were far too removed from the day-to-day activities to ensure a well-functioning indenture emigration system. The indenture system was too thinly spread out in many colonies in the Indian Ocean and the Caribbean Sea for effective administration. Subsequently, loopholes and weaknesses in the system were exploited by the recruiters in India and the planters in the Caribbean. In India, the recruiters were merely interested in meeting the quota of emigrants rather than obeying recruitment policies. Women were particularly targeted since about 40 percent of them were needed before a ship could leave the ports in India. The situation became worse when the authorities raised the fee for the recruitment of women with the expectation that more women would be added to the migration pool. Instead, the recruiters began forcing Indian women to labor overseas against their will. The Sanderson Commission reported that the recruiting staffs were very corrupt and that they were paid for results, by the number of recruits they obtained. The consequence was that recruiters were very often successful in enticing single women as well as married women—who left their husbands—to serve indenture. Local magistrates in India often declared that all kinds of riffraff were granted licenses as recruiters. Yearly immigration reports revealed that at least 5 percent of recruiting licenses were revoked. In 1900, for example, 1,088 recruiters were given licenses and twenty-seven were cancelled. The numbers and reasons for cancellation are provided in table 2.

In the Caribbean, planters had enormous power over most political matters, even over the protectors of emigrants, who were often seen socializing

TABLE 2: REASONS FOR RECRUITMENT LICENSE REVOCATIONS	
No. revoked	**Reason**
7	Working for other agencies
4	Fraud
3	Bad character
2	Insufficient accommodation for intending emigrants
2	Kidnapping
1	Theft
1	Detaining unwilling emigrants
1	Wrongfully restraining a woman
1	Found unfit to hold a recruitment license
1	Assaulting emigrants
1	Misconduct
1	Making false statements
1	No permanent residence and no one to certify character
1	Duping a woman into indenture

Source: *Report on Emigration from the Port of Calcutta to British and Foreign Colonies, 1900, Protector of Emigrants* (Calcutta: Bengal Secretariat Press, 1901).

with the planters, indicating that they had more commonality with the planter class than with the laboring class they were supposed to protect. Worst of all was the fact that the laws favored the planter class. Look Lai writes eloquently:

There was also a systematic institutional deception entrenched in the whole system, in that no one ever informed the intending emigrant ... about the harsh disciplinary laws imposed unilaterally by the planter controlled colonial legislatures contained in the immigration ordinances, the whole apparatus of criminal penalties attached to small and large infractions of the contract or of basic work-discipline. This omission remained basic to the entire immigration experiment and thereby defined the indenture system as a quasi-servile labour system ... (1993, 79)

THE INDIAN EMIGRANTS:
GENDER, CASTE, RELIGION, AND LANGUAGE

Perhaps it should be stated that during indenture and even in the modern period, Indians were known as Coolies. The meaning of the word in India was not negative. It was simply used to describe someone who was a porter. In the Caribbean, however, the word meant stupid, backward, uncivilized, and resistant to change. What is interesting is that only the first batches of Indians who went to Mauritius in 1834 and to British Guiana in 1838 were Coolies, but the term was applied to all Indians who served indenture. Unfortunately, the psychological impact of this word on Indians is yet to be fully assessed. Generally, the word was used to make Indians feel inferior and that they were capable only of providing menial labor. The planter class, however, declared openly that they wanted a predominantly young, male, "Coolie" labor force. Two main reasons were given for this preference. First, women were perceived to be a burden rather than a benefit to the patriarchal plantation system due to their role in childbearing and childcare. Second, the colonial officials claimed that it was difficult to entice Indian women to leave their homeland, even when higher commissions were offered to recruiters. These reasons were persuasive, so when indenture began in British Guiana, the ratio of men to women was one hundred to three. This pattern continued until the late 1850s, when social pathologies, in particular abuse and wife murders, started to erupt on the plantations because of the shortage of women. Indian males competed for fewer Indian females. The colonial authorities encouraged the recruitment of more women with good standing to nurture and nourish a stable environment for indentured Indians. Table 3 provides a sample of the ratio of men to women arriving in 1877, during the middle period of the indenture system.

The proportion of women to men varies from less than one half to a third or even less. Of the total of eight ships that brought Indians from India to British Guiana in 1877, 2,471 Indians were males while 974 were females. The ratio was two and a half men to one woman (2.5:1.0). Boys and girls comprised 276 individuals. A small number of boys and girls were probably recruited individually like adults, but the high number of individuals who were not adult men and women showed that during the middle years of indenture single emigrants had reduced substantially. Emigrants were going overseas as a family, although some children might have been born out of wedlock. However, more single women than married women were going to the Caribbean. Of the 2,808 women that were dispatched from

TABLE 3: MALE TO FEMALE COMPARISON FOR SHIPS FROM INDIA TO BRITISH GUIANA IN 1877					
Ship name	Voyage length (days)	Men	Women	Boys	Girls
Ailsa	81	296	128	29	11
Ailsa	99	304	125	18	14
Jura	100	337	154	21	8
King Arthur	101	321	93	15	10
Neva	85	275	121	30	15
Pandora	92	300	136	18	14
Rohilla	83	275	100	21	9
Shiela	98	363	117	19	24
Total		2,471	974	171	105

Source: British Guiana, "Immigration Agent General (IAG) Report of the Immigration Agent General for the Year 1877," in *The Argosy* (Georgetown, British Guiana: Demerara, 1888).

India to the colonies, including the Indian Ocean islands, in 1906, 1,224 were accompanied by their husbands, and the remaining 1,554, or 56.41 percent, were understood to be single women (see the 1906 *Report on Emigration from the Port of Calcutta to British and Foreign Colonies*). That a majority of single women migrated under whatever circumstances revealed that Indian women in the nineteenth century might have been under less control and social surveillance by their male-dominated social structure than previously thought.

Like gender, a brief assessment of the social structure of Indian emigrants is warranted to show how this once-significant aspect of cultural identity had become meaningless in the Caribbean. Indian emigrants were recruited from the four main castes within Hinduism: Brahmin (priests), Kishatriya (warriors and rulers), Vaishya (business and agricultural caste), and Sudras (menial caste). On the whole, the caste composition of the migrants recruited reflected somewhat the caste composition of India, which meant that more low- and middle-caste Indians were recruited to labor in the Caribbean. D. W. D. Comins (1893c) showed that of 3,072 Indians introduced in Trinidad during the season between 1889 and 1890 there were over forty types of castes. The largest numbers were from Chamar and Muhammadan, while the smallest numbers were from the Sandi and Bostom castes. While it is difficult to say precisely how many different castes were brought to the Caribbean since some Indians gave the immigration authorities the wrong caste to gain upward social mobility, more than two-thirds of the emigrants were

TABLE 4: CASTE AND RELIGION AMONG INDIAN EMIGRANTS TO THE CARIBBEAN IN 1901

Caste and religion	Demerara	Trinidad	Suriname	Total
Agriculturalist	763	769	309	1,917
Artisan	161	141	109	411
Christians	0	0	2	2
Hindus, Brahmins, High Castes	174	353	228	755
Low caste	524	689	385	1,598
Muslims	352	389	229	970

Source: *Report on Emigration from the Port of Calcutta to British and Foreign Colonies, 1901, Protector of Emigrants* (Calcutta: Bengal Secretariat Press, 1902).

from the low caste. Over time, however, the caste structure did not survive in the Caribbean, mainly because of the capitalist nature of the plantation system. Caste doctrines were not considered in the daily routine of work and life. Of all Indian customs, the caste did not survive the crossing from India to the Caribbean plantations.

Like caste, the religious composition of the emigrants also mirrored the religious breakdown of India, with 84 percent of migrants being Hindu and 16 percent being Muslim or other religions. The annual report on emigration for the year 1901 shows in table 4 that a majority of the emigrants to the Caribbean that year were from a Hindu background. Of all the emigrants, low-caste Hindus constituted 65 percent; high-caste, 12 percent; middle-caste, 7.2 percent; and Muslims, 15 percent, while women made up about a third of emigrants.

These emigrants were recruited from various areas in north and south India and therefore spoke a variety of regional languages. Researcher Steven Vertovec (1992) found that during the indenture period in Trinidad Indians spoke Bengali, Punjabi, Hindu, Urdu, Oriya, Nepali, Gujerati, Telugu, Tamil, Oraons, Santals, Vanga, Radha, Varendra, Rajbangshi, Magahi, Maithili, Shadri, Awadhi, Bhojpuri, Eastern and Western Hindi, Bangaru, Ajmeri, and Tondai Nadu. Over time, however, Bojpuri in Trinidad, Sarnami in Suriname, and various forms of Caribbean Creole became the main languages of communication among Indians. All the other languages have experienced a uniform death. The stop of the flow of fresh indentured Indians since 1917, the preference for the English language and Creole in the education system, and prerequisites for secure employment as well as the continuous migration to Europe and North America have marginalized and drowned out the use of Indian languages on a daily basis.

THE SEA JOURNEY FROM INDIA TO THE CARIBBEAN

The sea journey actually began in the depots. Much has been written about the cultural aspects of the depots: caste, religion, the diversity of the emigrants, and how they formed makeshift unions of brotherhood and sisterhood to console, cohere, and coexist in times of hardship. Less known are the physical and psychological conditions. While these conditions improved over time, they were never completely eliminated. Sanitation was poor and diseases and deaths were always present. In 1906, for example, of the twenty thousand intending emigrants in the Calcutta depots waiting to be transported to various overseas colonies, there were three cases of cholera and two deaths; eight cases of small pox; eleven cases of chicken pox; 173 cases of measles and fifteen deaths; 455 admissions for fever and eight deaths; eighty-one cases of cerebrospinal meningitis and forty-one deaths; 261 admissions for respiratory diseases and thirty-five deaths; and twenty-eight infants who died and twenty-six who were born. Women gave birth on every ship that left India to the Caribbean, which indicated that the authorities were not very concerned about the dangers associated with birth on the high seas. Some women who boarded the ships were visibly pregnant since some births happened during the first half of the normal months-long journey. But more importantly, Indian women giving birth on the sea voyages revealed their willingness to take risks. Why were they willing to travel over high seas while pregnant? Were they so desperate for a better life? Were some of them fleeing to conceal their unplanned pregnancy to avoid social expulsion? Were some women leaving on the wishes of the family? Whatever might have been the case, their willingness to travel while pregnant exemplified courage, a cultural characteristic they took with them to the Caribbean plantations (Roopnarine 2010).

The sea voyage from India to the Caribbean is about eleven thousand miles. Nineteenth-century wooden sailing ships would make this journey in about four to five months, or just over one hundred days. After the introduction of iron steamships in the 1870s, the same journey was completed in about three months. In 1877, for example, the ship *Ailsa* left India on November 5 and arrived in British Guiana on January 28, 1878, a total of eighty-one days. Ships normally travelled an average of 1,176 miles per week, 168 miles per day, and seven miles per hour. If the weather was bad, the voyage could potentially be longer. Most ships left India during August and March, when the weather was more favorable. Ships from the Indian Ports of Calcutta and Madras generally travelled through the Bay of Bengal and around the

Cape of Good Hope and stopped at St. Helena to pick up fresh water and food, if needed, before continuing to the Caribbean islands.

The ship crew was a diverse group of individuals from different nationalities and occupational backgrounds. Crew members were ranked according to occupational status. The most important individual on the ship was the surgeon-superintendent, not the captain. He was a male appointed by the protector of immigrants. The surgeon was responsible for the medical inspection of the migrants, proper ventilation and cooking arrangements, hospital space, and food storage. He kept a list of all the passengers, including the crew, and documented all significant events, such as births and deaths, as well as unexpected events (abuse, rape, revolts) that occurred onboard the ship. The surgeon was paid according to how many Indians landed alive. There was also the third mate, who was the surgeon's right-hand man but reported to the captain of the ship. The third mate was customarily the ship's safety officer, responsible for discipline among the emigrants. Below the third mate were the compounders, who were druggists, dispensers of medicine as well as mediators (mainly Indian mediators). They were the intermediaries between European and Indian passengers onboard the ship. They possessed some knowledge of European languages and customs as well as of the Indian passengers. In the lower ranks were the *sirdars* (headmen), *bandharries* (native cooks), and *topazes* (sweepers). These individuals were Indians, but their duties varied. Each *sirdar* was responsible for twenty-five Indian passengers to ensure proper conduct and order onboard the ship, while *bandharries* were drawn from the upper caste to avoid any suspicion of caste contamination. The *topazes* held the lowest rank among the crew and came from a low caste. They were responsible for sweeping and cleaning the ship.

Every sea voyage was guided by nineteen detailed clauses or rules. They were chiefly related to contracts, numbers of emigrants, penalties if contract terms were not carried out, the seaworthiness, staffing, and deck space of ships, the availability of clean water, access to a trained surgeon and medicines, and the proper treatment of migrants. In spite of these regulations, for a majority of Indians the sea voyage was a lonely and uncertain experience. Like in the depots, fear, births, deaths, diseases, depression, suicide, and abuse (especially of women) were common onboard the ships bound for the Caribbean. Cholera, typhoid, dysentery, scurvy, scorbutic diarrhea, and beriberi broke out very often on ships. Although deaths varied from ship to ship and from time to time, they were a common feature on every ship. In 1856–57, 4,094 Indians were taken from Calcutta to the Caribbean in twelve

TABLE 5: VOYAGE MORTALITY RATES FROM INDIA TO THE CARIBBEAN, 1860–61

Destination	No. ships	No. embarked	No. deaths	Mortality percent
British Guiana	8	3,152	128	4.0
Grenada	2	802	22	2.7
Jamaica	3	1,057	131	12.3
St. Lucia	1	336	17	5.0
St. Vincent	1	308	10	3.2
Trinidad	5	2,023	71	3.4

Source: British Parliamentary Papers, *The Twenty-second General Report of the Colonial Land and Emigration Commissioners* (London: Irish University Press, 1862), 49.

different ships. Of this number, 707 Indians died, an average mortality rate of 17.27 percent. On one ship, the mortality rate was 31.17 percent (British Parliamentary Papers 1874, 23–24). Table 5 shows that the death rate on ships leaving India for the Caribbean between 1860 and 1861 ranged from 2 percent to 12 percent.

In 1877, of the total of 3,905 emigrants taken to British Guiana, eighty-four perished, including fourteen infants. Deaths on the voyages were reduced toward the end of indenture due to improvements in management and facilities. In 1904, of the 7,135 intending indentured emigrants taken to various colonies on eleven ships, twenty-one, or 0.39 percent, perished, deaths that occurred mainly on ships bound for British Guiana (see the 1904 *Report on Emigration from the Port of Calcutta to British and Foreign Colonies*). Deaths on the sea voyage were inevitable events that accompanied indenture emigration. Why were there so many deaths among the passengers? Newborns, infants, and children were naturally unprepared for the long voyage to the Caribbean. Their parents and guardians were certainly under duress from the tumultuous sea voyage and were not prepared to deal with the additional stress of taking care of younger ones in need. Some young ones died simply from neglect and poor medical attention. Some intending indentured Indians were recruited from impoverished sectors of Indian society and were therefore unfit to endure the long sea voyage. Some were so depressed from the sea voyage that they allowed themselves to die instead of seeking treatment. Others committed suicide. In spite of the dangers associated with the sea voyage, Indian emigrants continued to indenture themselves overseas.

Chapter Two

INDIAN MIGRATION DURING THE INDENTURED PERIOD

The previous chapter examined the movement of Indians from India to the Caribbean—commonly known as indentured emigration—between 1838 and 1917. This chapter continues to analyze Indian migration during indenture, primarily from when Indians arrived on the plantations to when their contractual obligations expired. The focus will be on indentured Indians who were under contract as well as those who stayed on after their contracts expired but within the overall time frame of indenture. The argument is that Indians were brought to the Caribbean under a series of restrictive colonial policies that stymied free movement. However, it is also argued that some Indians resisted these colonial regulations and exercised their right to migrate. Fewer Indians migrated illegally than remained on the plantations. Nonetheless, illegal migration was a permanent feature of the plantation system that lasted as long as indenture itself. This chapter divides Indian migration during indenture into three overlapping historical phases: (1) illegal migration in the form of desertion from the plantations; (2) migration from the plantations to rural settlements to urban areas; and (3) intraregional migration from one Caribbean country to another. Illegal migration did occur in the latter two migration phases but was more prominent in the first phase in the form of desertion.

CONCEPTIONS OF MIGRATION DURING INDENTURE

The scholarship on Indian migration during indenture mainly focuses on restriction. Indentured servants were subjected to a battery of labor ordinances and laws that locked them within a two-mile radius of their assigned plantations. They had little or no opportunity for migration, not only because of the stern labor ordinances but also because they were very unfamiliar with their new surroundings, at least during the first six to twelve months upon arrival in the Caribbean. They were simply unaware of migration opportunities beyond their plantation base and therefore complied with the colonial codes of indenture. There is little dispute among scholars that indentured laborers were discouraged from engaging in migration. According to their contracts, they were to be transported to the Caribbean to work and to return home when their work assignments were completed. From all practical indications based on previous studies, their migration was between India and the Caribbean. The colonial indenture system ensured that the indentured Indians would obey this pattern of migration or surrender to the demands of their contracts. The question is, were indentured Indians really locked into their plantation base? Did they remain on a specific plantation for five years? Did they simply obey labor ordinances with regard to migration? Were their indentured lives wholly based on work and confinement? Emerging literature shows that when the laboring class is suppressed or when their aspirations for a better life with regard to basic rights, wages, and overall treatment are denied, they will use any means possible, including migration, to improve their circumstances. James Scott (1990; 1985), Gayatri Spivak (1988), Michel Foucault (1972), and others argue that the subaltern was able to speak back to power through insurgency and resistance because they were the agents of change who drew upon their own day-to-day experience to challenge structural domination. The subaltern approach has brought a dialectical interest to the static view of elite historiography with its assumptions of backwardness and underdevelopment of the masses. Likewise, a case can be developed for the indentured Indians in the Caribbean by arguing that, although they were traditional, communal people, they were also competitive individuals seeking their own destiny within the confines of a controlled plantation system. Within this restrictive colonial power structure, they created innovative ways to migrate and improve their lives.

Studies on how Indians used migration and even resisted the indenture system to benefit their lives are very rare in Indo-Caribbean scholarship. Their preindenture history and plantation experience in dealing with domination have rarely been acknowledged. Until recently, there has been little discussion on the agency, resistance, and power indentured Indians possessed in their everyday actions and interactions, on and beyond the plantations. Their indenture experience has been lampooned in Indian-Caribbean historiography as they've been portrayed as victims of a paternalistic plantation system where ideological and institutional forms of domination prevailed. This chapter challenges these views and argues that indentured Indians used migration within the confines of the indenture system to improve their lives and turn situations and circumstances to their advantage. Specifically, they sought out the weakest links in the indenture system and manipulated them to benefit themselves. Indentured Indians carved out, when possible, some measure of independence for themselves inside and outside the plantation system. In the former case, some indentured Indians worked with the system until their contracts expired before exercising their right to migrate, while in the latter case, the more militant indentured immigrants resorted to defiant measures to acquire freedom of movement, however illegally. These dynamics added to the complexity of Indian migration during indenture. Some Indians migrated following colonial regulations, while others defied these regulations.

DESERTION AS A FORM OF MIGRATION

When Indians arrived on the plantations they were already aware that the indenture labor system would not be what they had expected. Their depot and sea voyage experience impressed upon them that indenture meant providing hard and continuous labor to plantations. To ensure that indentured Indians complied with labor expectations, special ordinance laws were developed and designed to forestall the movement of Indians away from the plantations to independent survival. One specific ordinance states that all immigrants were required to produce or carry a certificate of exemption from labor or a free certificate to distinguish between laborers and deserters or absconders. Indian Immigration Ordinance No. 135 stated that every indentured immigrant should remain on the plantation to which he or she was indentured. If an indentured Indian was found outside of his residential plantation and failed to produce a pass, he was arrested and taken to the nearest police station (British Parliamentary Papers 1904, 30). According to Ordinance No. 140, a deserter was someone who absented himself without leave for three days from the plantation where he was indentured. Put simply, a deserter was an indentured laborer who left his or her assigned plantation for three consecutive days without informing his or her boss or asking for permission (32). In this context, desertion is a form of migration since it represents a movement away from one environment to another. Arguably, what matters is not the distance but the conditions in which the movement

TABLE 6: INDENTURED INDIAN DESERTION RATES IN INDIA, 1901–05			
Year	No. registered for indentured labor	No. who deserted on the journey to Calcutta depot	No. who deserted from the Calcutta depot
1901	17,750	42	265
1902	13,807	13	113
1903	12,403	51	102
1904	10,286	52	103
1905	15,296	17	32
Total	69,542	176	615

Source: *Report on Emigration from the Port of Calcutta to British and Foreign Colonies* for the years 1901–05 (Calcutta: Bengal Secretariat Press, 1902; 1903; 1904; 1905; 1906).

occurred. Some indentured Indians were reacting to their inflexible labor contracts through flight to seek better livelihood opportunities, but from the point of view of the plantation managerial staff, desertion was illegal and carried the penalty of five pounds in fines or two months in prison, or both. The fine of five pounds was a substantial amount of money during indenture since the indentured daily wage was twenty-four cents for men and ten cents for women on average, a difference determined by assigned workload. In most cases, women performed lighter tasks than men and therefore received lower wages, although one cannot dismiss the fact that the plantation system regarded women's labor as secondary to that of men. The fine of five pounds had an enormous impact on the mentality of the indentured, which explains why desertions were not as frequent as would be expected in a paternal plantation system. During indenture, one pound was worth four dollars and eighty cents, which meant five pounds was equal to about twenty-four dollars. If an indentured man was fined five pounds, he had to work one hundred days to pay off his fine. In contrast, if a woman was fined five pounds, she had to work two hundred and forty days to pay off her fine. This explains why deserters never returned to their former plantation base. The deserters made sure they would never be caught because of the draconian nature of the fines. However, desertion did not mean freedom because deserters often entered into other forms of exploitation with their new bosses, as discussed below.

A majority of indentured Indians stayed on the plantations to serve out their contracts and then migrated to other plantations or nonplantation areas for employment opportunities. But a smaller number of indentured Indians were not as dedicated and abandoned their contractual indenture obligations.

TABLE 7: INDENTURED INDIAN DESERTION RATES IN THE CARIBBEAN		
Colony	Years	No. deserted
British Guiana	1865–1890	13,988
Martinique	1862–1874	741
Jamaica	1910–1921	340
Dutch Guiana	1876–1917	327
Total		15,126

Source: Lomarsh Roopnarine, "Indian Migration during Indentured Servitude in British Guiana and Trinidad, 1850–1920," *Labor History* 52, no. 2 (2011): 178.

They were willing to breach or violate their contracts to achieve independent survival. From the standpoint of indentured Indians, this movement was illegal but justifiable. To some indentured Indians, the overall system offered few opportunities for personal and family development for those who were constrained. To individuals living in such a state of servitude, the mere idea of desertion offered an escape from the yoke of labor obligations to a new environment with the expectation of a new beginning, however challenging. In this regard, desertion was a form of migration based on the desire for freedom and the power to dictate one's own time. The movement was a natural reaction to the drudgery and hazards of plantation life. Evidence for desertion first appears in India. Table 6 provides information on desertion rates of intending indentured Indians for five years.

The purpose of table 6 is to show that even though deserters were a small fraction of the registered emigrants, desertion occurred continuously throughout indenture. If we make a conservative estimate that at least one hundred intending indentured Indians deserted every year during seventy years of indenture, then no less than seven thousand would have deserted before embarkation in India. It is important to emphasize the aforesaid movement because it has remained an undiscussed aspect of indenture that continued throughout indenture in the Caribbean. Desertion was higher in the Caribbean than in India. Table 7 shows desertion statistics in selected Caribbean colonies during indenture.

Who were these deserters? The deserters were essentially indentured servants from various backgrounds. Little information exists, however, on the age and gender of the deserters. It would have been interesting to know how many deserters were women since this statistic could potentially reopen or even reposition the argument on whether women were subservient or subversive indentured servants. The records show that deserters were both first arrivals, known also as casuals, and seasoned emigrants. The argument can be made that the first arrivals were more inclined to desert because some were recruited under false pretenses (having been duped or lured) and were ill suited to perform hard agricultural plantation work. Whenever possible, these Indians deserted because they did not have much to lose. They understood that there was no possibility of negotiation with their plantation bosses and simply chose flight to restore their preindenture lifestyle or create one that was an alternative to the plantation system. Likewise, seasoned emigrants were cognizant of the options open to them beyond the plantations because they had been in the colonies for a long time. What is most striking is the regional differences: The majority of deserters were Madras emigrants. To review, they were recruited from South India and constituted the numerical minority of emigrants brought to the Caribbean. Their lifestyles were markedly different from those of the North Hindu Indians. They did not live according to the dharma and karma principles of Hinduism. Rather, they preferred a more liberal lifestyle, free from confinement and regular work routine. When this lifestyle was disturbed, they resisted and eventually deserted plantation work. From 1845 to 1848, an estimated 3,985 Madras emigrants were brought to British Guiana, and of this number 1,249, or 33.5 percent, died or deserted the plantations. By comparison, 3,668 North Indians were brought to British Guiana during the same period and only 265, or 7.2 percent, disappeared from the plantations (Roopnarine 2011, 179). Many of the Indians who disappeared ended up as beggars in urban areas, especially around Bourda Market in Georgetown, British Guiana.

Why did indentured servants desert the plantations, considering that they were perceived by their plantation bosses to be docile people who were inclined to stay on the plantations and provide labor to their employer? The question of desertion becomes more puzzling considering that indentured servants were in the Caribbean on a temporary basis to work and return home. Why would they want to violate their contractual agreements and migrate illegally to unknown destinations far from their homeland? Their desire to desert the plantations was most likely connected to the conditions under which they lived and worked. First, to the deserters, migration was a natural reaction to the drudgery and hazards of plantation life. The death rates among British Guianese Indians from 1908 to 1911 were 32.6 percent, 33.7 percent, 37.6 percent, and 32.1 percent, respectively (British Parliamentary Papers 1910a, 64). These rates were higher than the death rates among all ethnic groups. High death rates occurred because the colonial indenture system was designed largely for the economic interests of the planter class. Premature deaths among indentured Indians were seen as a natural part of the indenture system. Second, desertion was encouraged by the proximity of the Caribbean islands to each other, Venezuela to Trinidad, and British Guiana's forested terrain. These natural environments provided opportunities for desertion. Moreover, the deserters recognized that the planters were handicapped by the very environment they sought to conquer and colonize. British Guiana's forested terrain, in particular, proved too cumbersome an obstacle for the planters to deal with desertion. They simply allowed some desertion to occur. To the deserters, any movement away from planters' control offered an opportunity for an alternative way of life, and the forest provided a safe hideout from recapture. Some deserters, however, found regular employment with the interior Amerindians in British Guiana and cocoa farmers in Venezuela, but they were not totally free from exploitation. They entered into new forms of exploitation as their new employers took advantage of their illegal status by withholding wages and threatening to return them to their former employers.

What happened to the deserters? Some were captured, while others became vagrants in urban areas. They were the eyesore of the indenture system that the planters wanted to avoid. The planter class regarded homelessness and insanity among the deserters as the fault of the deserters rather than the fault of the pitiless plantation system. The deserters were never successful in forming permanent communities like the Maroons in Jamaica and Suriname during slavery. The pattern of desertion was (1) more individualistic than collective, (2) more reactionary to plantation conditions than preplanned, and (3) more consistent though relatively smaller in number than those who remained on the plantations. The practice of desertion as a form of migration is evidence that some Indians were not willing to be cowed into indenture, even when they signed indenture contracts (see Mahase 2008). Their desire to desert showed a considerable degree of determination to live autonomous lives against tremendous odds. Some had a strong sense of pride in their ability to acquire "freedom" in a new environment that was designed to control them.

RURAL-URBAN MIGRATION DURING INDENTURE, 1870s–1917

Legal rural-urban migration during indenture began in the 1860s and 1870s, mainly in colonial Trinidad and British Guiana (see Potter 1975). The impetus for rural-urban migration was the colonial policy of offering Indians small parcels of land to settle in exchange for their right to return passages to their homeland. The planter class reasoned that it would be cheaper for them to have Indians settle around vacant plantation lands rather than to send them back to an impoverished environment in India when their contracts expired. It was believed that the Indians would be happy to acquire land for the first time in their lives, a win-win situation for the planters as well as for the Indian settlers. For example, in British Guiana, the amount paid to return former indentured immigrants from 1850 to 1870 was $478,217. In Jamaica, the cost for returning Indians from that colony between 1891 and 1895 was $109,000 (Roopnarine 2008, 212). While the cost to send former indentured Indians back to their homeland seemed expensive, a closer examination revealed that it cost the planters more to settle Indians locally than to send them back home. In latter stages of indenture in Jamaica, the cost to bring in one indentured individual was around $58, and the cost to send that same individual back to his homeland after indenture was around $14. It is important to also take into consideration that by the 1880s Indians had to contribute financially to their own return passage. Males contributed one-half the cost, while females contributed one-third to their return passage. Moreover, only a third of indentured servants returned to their homeland. The idea of settling Indians on vacant lands, then, had more to do with the objective of retaining a regular supply of cheap labor for the plantation system than accommodating the Indian laborers.

The land settlement schemes turned out to be a failure. The overall planning and executing of the scheme was deficient. The arrangement for water supplies and the maintenance of drainage systems were inadequate and unsuitable. The lands were either too far from the base of Indian communities or were too close to the sugar estates, serving the interests of the planters rather than those of the settlers. For the most part, the lands granted were infertile and unfit for easy cultivation. A lack of a real sense of community among the thousands of settlers, a lack of experience with land ownership, and a lack of knowledge on how to upkeep the land stymied any sound development. Consistent guidance from the government on how to utilize the land efficiently and effectively was sadly absent. The government officials withdrew too early after the allotment distribution. Worst of all, the planters were reluctant to allow Indians to choose their own allotments, mainly to prevent competition with the sugar plantations; this option obviously would have defeated the purpose of introducing Indians in the Caribbean. Finally, confusion surrounded the land settlement schemes on matters relating to taxes, responsibility, and actual title and ownership. Sometimes land was allotted when it was already in someone else's name (Roopnarine 2008, 214–15).

In spite of land settlement scheme challenges in regard to successful community development and independent survival, Indians were able for the first time since their arrival in the Caribbean to break out of their insular plantation domains. Some were willing to move out of the former slave barracks to land settlements even with the inherent challenging conditions. To Indians, the land settlement schemes held possibilities for a gradual and better future compared to that of remaining on the plantation permanently. Actually, the mere movement from these barrack dwellings to anywhere else was a mark of progress—a phenomenon already noticed in the departure of slaves from plantation housing to independent survival. Two decades following the start of the land settlement schemes, an impressive movement of Indians from their plantation base was evident. In British Guiana, from 1872 to 1876, an estimated fifteen thousand Indians left the plantations and settled in Norten Zuill, Huist t'Dieren, Bush Lot, Whim, and Maria's Pleasure. The movement from the plantations to settlements continued gradually but impressively, and by 1911, 65,810 Indians out of a total population of 127,000 were living off the plantations. In 1871, 32 percent of Indians in Trinidad were living in villages and settlements, particularly in Montserrat Ward, Calcutta, Coolie Town, and Chaguanas (Roopnarine 2001, 7–8; Vertovec 1992, 95; Wood 1968, 275). By 1900, the number of Indians living on the plantations declined steadily and only 16,643 (19.9 percent) out of an Indian population of 85,615 were living on plantations (Ramesar 1994, 77). In Jamaica, more than half of the Indian population of thirty-six thousand moved off the plantations, mainly to Paul Island, Fellowship, and Race Course settlements (Shepherd 1994, 107). Indians from all backgrounds, including children and women, participated in this migration.

While the land settlements schemes were located not too far from the plantations and conditions on the lands initially were not that different from the indentured Indians' former plantation bases, land settlement schemes provided other opportunities. Indians were able to establish an economic base through an elastic relationship with the plantations and the land settle- ments. They worked on the plantations as well as in their own living environ- ment, particularly on vacant lands. What emerged in the land settlement schemes was a new culture as Indians engaged in rice planting, cattle and poultry rearing, grass cutting, trading, shop keeping, and money lending. Noticeable, too, was the re-creation and reconsolidation of their homeland culture. For example, Hinduism was widely practiced. Religious flags of red appeared in front of every Hindu home, signifying homage to their Hindu culture. Muharram festivals among Muslims were also practiced. Indians were, by the last decades of indenture, starting to feel rather comfortable in the Caribbean. Not only did their population grow but also they were able to experience some level of economic prosperity and cultural confidence in their new environment. This development created two different events with regard to migration. First, it stymied Indian return migration to their homeland and migration from land settlements to urban areas. A majority of Indians simply became comfortable with rural life, which in many ways was similar to that of their homeland in climate and peasant life. Rural India, where many of the emigrants came from, and the Caribbean share the same warm, tropical climate. Like in rural India in the nineteenth century, peasant residences around the Caribbean plantations used oil lamps, which, although inadequate, never created misery. Moreover, Indians found rural life safe, and they had the opportunity to own land and experience collective rather than individualistic attributes of culture. These rural Indians were not interested in the modernization of their social and economic structure, although they made some changes such as adopting Western education. They were more interested in interdependence among themselves, their communities, and, when necessary, their new environment. This is how they had lived historically in India, focusing more on the preservation of rural life through the celebration of festivals and the practice of folkways and mores without losing sight of the fact that their culture would be touched and affected by Western influence. Also, the comfort and confidence of rural life spawned new interests among some Indians. They did not want simply to stick with rural life but to explore other opportunities beyond their village through migration, principally to urban areas, in their own resident colonies.

The movement from rural to urban areas followed a step migration, that is, Indians moved first from the plantations to settlements and then to urban areas, although some moved directly from the plantations to urban areas. The latter movement was always less common and more irregular than the movement from the settlements to urban areas. The rural-urban movement was based on economic success and individual aspirations. As some Indians experienced steady progress and accumulated wealth, they transferred their economic activities to urban areas. During the last decade of indenture and after, their presence became very visible in Georgetown, Guyana; Port-of-Spain, Trinidad; Kingston, Jamaica; and Paramaribo, Suriname, as they became shop owners selling drugs, spirits, and provisions; pawnbrokers; or even milk and vegetable venders. Indians, especially women, could be seen in these urban areas carrying baskets of vegetables on their heads and milk cans slung over their shoulders, selling these items from door to door (Barros 1997; Shepherd 1986; Tyson 1939). By contrast, individual aspirations for rural-urban migration showed a different pattern. Some Indians were able to transfer their economic success from rural to urban areas with relative ease, although they had to compete with other ethnic groups, which resulted in ethnic tensions. Other Indians were able to move from their rural base because of Christian religious influence. Christian missionaries offered rural Indians opportunities for Western education. While this form of education was met with resistance from Hindu community leaders for intruding into their faith, a small number of, mostly young, males were allowed to attend Christian-administered schools and received Christian religious teachings and Western forms of education. This exposure to Western education and skills prompted Indians to seek stable opportunities beyond their rural agricultural belt. They were now prepared to compete for urban-oriented jobs in the civil service and private sectors; jobs that offered year-round stability compared to the seasonal employment and lower wages of rural jobs.

The rural-urban movement produced two identifiable outcomes. The first was the visibility of well-to-do Indians as well as those who engaged in middle- and low-income occupations. Anthropologist Johan Speckmann (1965, 43) writes that in Suriname from 1915 to 1920 Indians began to move to urban areas like Paramaribo and made their livings as porters, gardeners, day laborers, market traders, tailors, shopkeepers, and goldsmiths. Some were even beggars—a lifestyle frowned upon in the Caribbean but not in India. In India, begging is a socially accepted way of life, especially if it is guided by the Hindu belief of abandoning the urge for materialism and instead focusing on spiritualism. In the Caribbean, begging is perceived to indicate a weakness possessed by the beggar. The second outcome was a small but steady movement from the countryside to urban areas among those who stayed. This pattern has not changed significantly in some Caribbean countries like Guyana. Most of the Indians in Guyana are still rurally based. To illustrate, in 1911 in British Guiana, only 5.7 percent of the population of 126,000 Indians lived in urban areas. In 1921 in Trinidad the urban population among Indians was 6 percent (Ramesar 1994, 132). In 1943, 18.9 percent of the Jamaican Indian population lived in urban areas (Shepherd 1998 170). A similar movement occurred in Suriname (see Speckmann 1965). However, E. Moutoussamy noticed that urbanization was never popular among Indians in the French Caribbean (1989, 28).

Why were Indians so reluctant to live in urban areas? Or why were they so comfortable living in rural areas? To answer these questions, a brief examination of their lives in India and the circumstances in the Caribbean is warranted. Indentured Indians were recruited from mostly rural areas in India and lived lives that were essentially traditional, where bonds of kinship and the sentiment of togetherness were the norm. When they arrived in the Caribbean, they were placed in isolated rural plantations similar to their departed homeland in terms of ecology and population density. Put differently, the indentured simply exchanged one form of rural lifestyle and area for another. Over time, they were able to reconstruct their homeland culture, which in effect provided a deep anchorage for stability, security, and comfort with rural life. Many of the Indian plantation communities in the Caribbean were reconstructions of rural India. In some ways, this sense of rural comfort stymied rural-urban migration. Many in their community were not prepared to deal with aspects of life outside of rural areas. For instance, many were too uneducated and unskilled to take up employment opportunities in urban areas that required some exposure to Western education, accoutrement, and mannerism. Rural comfort also reinforced Indian social conservativeness. Girls, in particular, were not allowed to go to school, at least not Western-oriented schools, for fear that they might deviate from the traditional role of marrying an Indian man and performing wifely duties such as raising children and taking care of the family. The planter class was more than eager to abstain from interfering with the internal social dynamics of indentured Indians. The global compulsory Education Act was passed in 1876, but it was not enforced in Indian communities. Actually, special measures were taken to exempt Indian children from the education act (see Bacchus 1989, 160–61). The reason behind the exemption was that Indian children were needed more on the plantations than in schools to produce for their overlords as well as bring in supplemental income to the family.

Arguably, Indians were aware of the challenges involved in making a livelihood beyond their rural base. They realized that the Caribbean was an environment that was highly segregated according to ethnicity, color, race, and social status, as they themselves had experienced in isolated plantation communities. The question they might have asked themselves was, why leave a comfortable rural community for another unknown environment, one that would potentially place them in residential segregation, change their close-knit social relations, and have them exist in anonymity? Rural Indians felt no urgent need to give up primary relations for secondary ones, spontaneous expressions for impersonal ones, and some sense of rural comfort for urban stress. For some, moving from a rural to an urban setting was a second rupture from home after leaving India, an attack on their collective identity and culture and an unnecessary self-imposed burden on their lives. This view of urbanization among Indians changed after the 1960s.

INTRA-CARIBBEAN MIGRATION DURING INDENTURE

The general pattern of migration between the islands during the period of discussion from 1838 to 1917 was mostly Afro-Caribbean oriented. Since emancipation in 1838, a large number of Africans were pushed out of their island base because of limited opportunities and subsequently pulled by the need for labor in other islands. The movement was most noticeable from densely populated Barbados and Windward islands to the large plantations and gold mines in Trinidad, British Guiana, and Suriname, respectively. An estimated one hundred thousand Africans partook in this intraregional migration, with about fifty thousand going to British Guiana (see Rodney 1977). Indians participated in this migration phase by providing labor to the plantations and mines. The movement was small when compared to the African movement, mainly because a majority of Indians were tied to their indenture contracts and their new communities. The early intraregional movement laid the foundation for further movement, which was always small but had been steady ever since Indians arrived in the Caribbean. In some ways, the movement represented the first major attempt by Indians to break out of their insular island environment, which demonstrated an attempt to move from a dependent and passive peasantry into an independent, active peasantry. The movement was essentially an intracolonial affair; that is, migration occurred from one colony to another or from one underdeveloped area to another. The movement was pushed and pulled by government regulations, marginal economic opportunities, and aspirations for cultural connection.

The strict government-regulated indenture system spawned illegal migration from one island to the next. As during the rural-urban migration, some Indians challenged or ignored their contractual agreements with their employers and migrated to other islands in search of employment. They were encouraged by the fact that Africans were engaged in intraregional migration. Some even followed patterns of intraregional migration similar to the Africans. The proximity of the islands and countries also encouraged migration. Some Indians migrated from Plantation Skeldon in British Guiana to New Nickerie, a nearby town on the banks of the Corentyne River in Suriname, as well as from coastal plantation regions in the Guianas to interior regions, which in some ways were like a different country, given the terrain and distance from the plantations. Illegal intraregional migration also occurred from Trinidad to the coca plantations in northern Venezuela. The size of this illegal migration is not precisely known, but it was continuous during indenture. The mainstream movement, however, was legal.

Jamaican historian Verene Shepherd (1998, 173) writes that as soon as the contracts of the first batch of Indians that arrived in Jamaica in 1845 expired, they followed other postemancipation workers and migrated to Cuba. This movement makes sense because it coincided with the United States' capital investment in the sugar and coffee industries in the Spanish-speaking Caribbean: Cuba, the Dominican Republic, and Puerto Rico, which in turn attracted labor migrants from other areas of the Caribbean. In the first few decades of the twentieth century, an estimated three thousand Indians from Jamaica migrated to Cuba (Ramdin 2000, 261; Sarusky 1989). The movement of time-expired Indians among islands during indenture occurred almost everywhere that Indians were indentured. By the 1860s, Indians were migrating from the Windward Islands to British Guiana and Trinidad; from St. Kitts and Nevis to Danish St. Croix; from the 1870s, from British Guiana to Suriname and between British Guiana and Trinidad; from the 1880s, from Belize to Jamaica; and from the 1890s to 1920s, mostly from British Guiana to Suriname (Roopnarine 2003). Surinamese historian Hans Ramsoedh, based in the Netherlands, claims that in the 1870s many Indians from British Guiana migrated to New Nickerie, Suriname, and became small-scale farmers (2015; see also Gordijn 1977, 276). Why the colonial government allowed Indians to migrate and why Indians chose to migrate demonstrates the changing aspects of a strict labor system. To recall, the general policy toward migration after Indians arrived in the Caribbean was that they should finish their contracts and return home. One of the ordinances of the Indian immigration policy stated that passports should not be given to indentured Indians in the colony and those who were brought in under immigrant funds. The consequences of aiding an indentured laborer to migrate from his plantation base to another island were severe, including fines and imprisonment. By the 1870s, Indians were given an option to settle by exchanging their return passage for a piece of land. Those who accepted land and settled still faced hardships and therefore opted to find employment outside the confines of the plantations. On some occasions, passports were given to time-expired Indians to migrate if they wished to remain in the Caribbean instead of returning to India. Surinamese historian Maurits Hassankhan stated that about twenty-five hundred Indian migrants went from British Guiana to Suriname during the period of indenture and until 1926. These migrants were integrated into the Hindustani community and became small-scale farmers (2015).

The Indian intra-Caribbean migration was not all based on providing manual labor. Some Indians migrated within the Caribbean islands for trading and educational purposes, although more research is needed to quantify the size and impact of these activities in the sending and receiving of colonies of Indians. What is certain is that they did travel, although on a temporary basis, for religious reasons. The impetus for this migration was largely influenced by Christian missionaries—mainly from Canada—in the Caribbean. To convert Indians to Christianity, the missionaries provided Western forms of education and badly needed social services to the Indian communities. Over time, their impact on Indian communities was very noticeable in areas of socioeconomic development and Christian-influenced education. However, the mission was met with opposition from Hindu and Muslim leaders for imposing on the general welfare of their children and community. The mission also faced internal challenges, particularly in reaching the Indian community at large. To get around this challenge, the mission promoted some Indians to the level of the priesthood and encouraged other Indians to become teachers and catechists. The aim was to use the experience of Indians to make the process of conversion to Christianity less cumbersome. What emerged from this program was that migratory Indians spread the doctrines of Christianity. Samaroo (1975, 93) espouses that from Trinidad the Christian mission was extended to Grenada in 1884 and to St. Lucia and British Guiana in 1885. In 1894 Indian pastors were sent to Jamaica to help the Presbyterian Church to reach indentured Indians. Similarly, Hindus and Muslims also sought to reinforce cultural religious beliefs among themselves, which in turn stimulated a modest intra-Caribbean migration among Indians.

Chapter Three

INDIAN MIGRATION
FROM THE CARIBBEAN TO INDIA

The previous chapter analyzed Indian migration during the period of in-denture. It argued that in spite of the restrictive measures against migration, Indians did engage in migration from the plantations to settlements to urban areas and to various islands in the Caribbean. The diversity of the move-ment demonstrates that Indians were more mobile than previously thought. They were not merely anchored to their assigned plantations. This chapter examines the final phase of Indian migration during indenture, essentially assessing the reasons Indians returned to their homeland in spite of incen-tives from the planter class to settle in the Caribbean. It also examines the amount of remittances the Indians took back with them. The assessment of remittances reveals whether or not the indenture system was beneficial to the laborers. This chapter focuses also on the underresearched movement of second-term immigrants, that is, Indians who had served indenture in the Caribbean and went back to India but chose to indenture for the second time in the Caribbean. The focus also extends to Indians who had served in other colonies—for example, in Fiji and Mauritius—and returned to India and then chose to come to the Caribbean. Even though indenture ended in 1920, the return migration of Indians continued until 1955, when the last ship left Georgetown, Guyana, with 255 Indians.

THE CHALLENGES OF RETURN MIGRATION FROM
THE CARIBBEAN TO INDIA

The reasons Indians went back to their homeland are multifaceted and complex. The entire premise of indentured labor was to fill the early postemancipation labor vacuum until a permanent labor force was found. Indians were brought to the Caribbean with the expectation of working the plantations for about three to five years and returning home. They were not expected to settle in the Caribbean. The Indian government also insisted on their return when their contracts expired so that they would not be abused outside the government's jurisdiction. The Indian government wanted the laborers to come back home so that other laborers could have the opportunity for employment. Finally, the Indian government wanted the laborers to come home with their remittances. The questions to be asked are these: What events led to the transformation of indenture from a temporary to a permanent labor system? Did the laborers have a say in this transformation? Were they duped twice, first in India to come to the Caribbean and, second, to stay in the Caribbean and become settlers? To illustrate, an estimated 500,000 were brought from India to the Caribbean, 175,000 returned to India, and 350,000 settled. These dynamics were not expected when the indenture system started in 1838, nor were they expected when the system was abolished in 1920. The transformation of the initial cyclical indenture system was directly related to the power of the planter class and the supposed weakness of colonial Indian government, which was under the tutelage of the British imperial government. To recall, the main aim of the planter class during the early postemancipation Caribbean was to secure the survival of the sugarcane industry, which meant pruning costs and achieving profits from the newly indentured labor force. They achieved both objectives, but to ensure stability both objectives had to be institutionalized. By the 1850s, the planters were confident enough to declare that Indian indentured labor was suitable and reliable because of the laborers' docility and industrious habits. The planter class argued that Indians should be given an option to re-indenture for another five years and receive a $50 bounty when their contracts expired. Indian laborers would not forfeit their right to a return passage. To laborers who had been living on the margins of society in India and the Caribbean, the planters' option was difficult to resist. Between 1850 and 1851, 2,210 Indians in British Guiana re-indentured and received bounties that totaled $107,410. In 1865 in Trinidad, 5,920 Indians re-indentured and received bounties that totaled $291.800 (British Parliamentary Papers 1866, 28). The planters' plan was so successful that in the late 1860s in Trinidad and the early 1870s in British Guiana they argued again for a change in the return policy, stating that the rights of return passage be exchanged for grants of land (about ten acres) in the Caribbean. In the late 1870s, the planters pushed again for a change in the policy of returning Indians to their homeland. They influenced colonial officials to change the laws to suit their needs. Law 12 of 1879, Section I, was introduced, which stated that returnees had to contribute one-fourth of the passage money in the case of males and one-sixth in the case of females. This law was subsequently amended by Law 2 of 1899, which increased the portion of passage money payable by immigrants to one-half in the case of males and one-third in the case of females. Destitute or disabled migrants with dependents were entitled to a free return passage (British Parliamentary Papers 1910a, Part II, Appendix, Jamaica, 75). This remained in effect until the end of the indenture system in 1920.

The planters' reason for the change of policy regarding sending back former indentured laborers was quite obvious. Sending indentured servants to their homeland was too expensive. They wanted Indians to stay around the plantations and provide continuous cheap labor. From the standpoint of the planter class, it made little sense to invest in indentured servants and send them back so quickly to an environment where their plantation experience was unsuitable. The continuous return of Indians was draining the labor market and required large sums of money. For example, in British Guiana, the amount paid for return passages of Indian immigrants from 1850 to 1870 was $478,217 (British Parliamentary Papers 1871, 183), and in Jamaica between 1891 and 1895, $109,000 was paid (Shepherd 1985, 21). The planters claimed that these sums of money should be invested in the Caribbean colonies, not India.

The planters' policy to have Indians remain in the Caribbean was successful, although some Indians stayed in the Caribbean because they wanted to. More than two-thirds of the laborers stayed while a third returned home. However, the number of Indians who returned declined substantially toward the end of indenture. Tables 8 and 9 provide a sample of arriving and departing Indian laborers in three colonies in 1911.

In tables 8 and 9, which represent marginally different statistics on Indian migration from 1900 to 1920, 5,012 laborers arrived in three Caribbean colonies and 166 left the same colonies in 1911. Less than 4 percent of laborers returned home. If this percentage of returning laborers were doubled or even tripled to cover margins of error, the return rate would still be less than half of the 33 percent who returned home in the earlier period. Three factors accounted for the reduction of returning laborers: the land inducement policy to settle; the responsibility on laborers to pay a part of their return passage; and the right in some colonies to use the return passage when so desired. There was no expiration date for the return passage, and some Indians simply delayed the prospect of going back home.

TABLE 8: LABORERS ARRIVING IN DEMERARA (BRITISH GUIANA), JAMAICA, AND TRINIDAD IN 1911

Colony	Men	Women	Children	Total
Demerara	1,349	558	142	2,049
Jamaica	538	217	40	795
Trinidad	1,472	567	129	2,168

Source: *Report on Emigration from the Port of Calcutta to British and Foreign Colonies, 1911, Protector of Emigrants* (Calcutta: Bengal Secretariat Press, 1912), appendix 3.

TABLE 9: LABORERS DEPARTING FROM DEMERARA (BRITISH GUIANA), JAMAICA, AND TRINIDAD IN 1911

Colony	Men	Women	Children	Total
Demerara	31	26	14	71
Jamaica	15	5	1	21
Trinidad	45	21	8	74

Source: *Report on Emigration from the Port of Calcutta to British and Foreign Colonies, 1911, Protector of Emigrants* (Calcutta: Bengal Secretariat Press, 1912), appendix 3.

THE TYPES OF RETURNEES AND REASONS FOR RETURNING TO INDIA

The former Indian indentured laborers who returned home were not a homogeneous group but differed in age, gender, and classification. For example, in 1911, out of 2,120 arrivals to British Guiana, 156 were under the age of ten; 441 were between eleven and twenty; 1,458 were between twenty-one and thirty; 45 were between thirty-one and forty; and no one was over forty (1911 *Report on Emigration from the Port of Calcutta to British and Foreign Colonies*, appendix VIII, 8). By contrast, in 1929 in British Guiana the *Sutlej* sailed from Georgetown to Calcutta carrying 520 persons, and the ages of these returnees were as follows: sixty-six under ten years old; sixty-one between eleven and twenty; twenty-six between twenty-one and thirty; 141 between thirty-one and forty; 129 between forty-one and fifty; seventy-five between fifty-one and sixty; and twenty-two over sixty years old. In sum, fewer children and older Indians were returning from the Caribbean (Immigration Agent General [hereafter IAG] 1930, 2). The gender or the ratio of the sexes among the returnees paralleled the pattern of arrivals; that is, fewer women than men arrived to and departed from the Caribbean, although the return numbers were much lower among women than their arrival numbers.

For example, in 1879, on the return ship *Malabar* from Georgetown, British Guiana, 331 men and 133 women sailed to Calcutta and Madras. There were one hundred men to forty-one women going back to Calcutta, while one hundred men to around sixty-eight women were returning to Madras. The ratio of the sexes was one hundred men to forty-two women (British Guiana 1881, 7). By 1907, fewer women were returning from the Caribbean to India. In that year, 466, 639, and 105 women left India and went to Demerara, Trinidad, and Jamaica, respectively, and eight, thirty-one, and eight, respectively, returned to India (British Guiana 1909, 1–4). The returning passengers were also diverse. The immigration agent report of 1929 in British Guiana shows that sixty-four Indians received free passage after ten years; 337 received assisted passage after ten years; twenty-two paid their own passage; and ninety-seven paupers were sent back free of charge (British Guiana 1930, 2). These statistics reveal some unexpected trends in the return migration. Even though indentured Indians were guaranteed a return passage when they left India, a majority of them had to pay a part of their return passage or were sent back by the colonial government. An astounding one-third of them were considered to be paupers on the ship *Malabar* in 1879. On every return ship from the Caribbean, at least 20 percent of the returnees were insane and paupers. A majority of them who returned were over the age of thirty, which meant they had arrived in the colonies at twenty and spent at least ten to fifteen years as indentured laborers before deciding to return to India. Finally, few women returned, indicating that they were becoming comfortable with the Caribbean.

The flow of returnees from the Caribbean to India never ceased. But why did a minority of Indians choose to return home when a majority of them remained in the Caribbean? They must have developed some significant relationships in the Caribbean, and therefore one is forced to ask, Did they sever relations for the second time, first when they left their homeland and, second, after living in the Caribbean for at least five years? Did they leave as single laborers or as families? Did they leave their families behind as they did in India? What was the mental state of these returnees? Why would women want to go back to an oppressive caste system? The first obvious reason why Indians returned to India was that many had a bad experience with the indenture system from recruitment in India to the sea voyage across the Indian and Atlantic Oceans to the Caribbean plantation. To these indentured Indians, life in the Caribbean was a miserable existence. They were just waiting for their contracts to expire to leave. The second reason was that there were indentured servants who had served their terms of contract either for their first or second term and were entitled by law to a free return passage, at least until the 1890s, to India. The third reason was that some former indentured Indians wished to return because they wanted only to use the indenture system to earn wages and did not develop any permanent attachments to the Caribbean. The fourth reason was that some former indentured servants came to the Caribbean to work and saved enough money to buy a piece of land and settle in their village in India. The fifth reason was that some former indentured laborers were transmigratory migrants; that is, they were aware that opportunities for indentured labor existed elsewhere. These former indentured laborers were returning home to contract themselves to another colony. The sixth reason was that paupers, invalids, and the infirm unfortunately had no other choice but to return since the colonies did not want them because they were economic liabilities, and, for the most part, they were entitled to a free passage back to India as stipulated in the labor contracts. The seventh reason was that some former indentured servants who were Hindus wanted to spend their last years meditating and eventually die in their homeland. Finally, some former indentured laborers mistakenly believed that India had gained independence in the 1920s, so they thought they were returning to a free India (Roopnarine 2006, 320).

REMITTANCES FROM INDENTURED INDIANS

The purpose of this section is to show the amount in remittances Indians took back with them to India to determine whether or not the indenture system was economically beneficial to the laborers. Structurally, it is important to analyze the context in which Indians accumulated savings to remit home in terms of wages earned and their sacrifice for and beyond the plantation system. For example, not all earned wages came from indenture contracts. Some Indians engaged in independent farming, shop keeping, and trading. The average wage for an able-bodied Indian male or female was one shilling or ten pence, respectively. These wages remained more or less constant on every indentured Caribbean colony during the course of indenture. Indians were obliged to work for seven to nine hours a day for 280 days per year. Indians earned more by working more rather than having increased wages. For example, if they were assigned to do six tasks and they finished that assigned work early, then they could take on more tasks for more wages. The following illustrates how much Indians were earning on a plantation in Trinidad from 1907 to 1908, a decade before indenture was abolished.

TABLE 10: INDENTURED INDIANS' RETURN WAGES EARNED ON BRECHIN ESTATES IN TRINIDAD, APRIL 1, 1907, TO MARCH 31, 1908

Gender	No.	Days worked	Total wages	Average wage per day
Male	461	280	$22,830.44	17.68 cents
Female	181	280	$3,512.85	6.93 cents

Source: British Parliamentary Papers, *Report of the Committee on Emigration from India to the Crown Colonies and Protectorates (Sanderson Commission)*, vol. 27, part 2 (Cd. 5192–94) (London: HMSO, 1910), 40 of appendix Trinidad.

TABLE 11: RETURNING IMMIGRANTS' JEWELRY DEPOSITS IN SURINAME, 1878–1911

Year	Ship name	No. men	No. women	No. children	Total	Amount to be returned in Calcutta	Estimated value
1878	Philosopher	265	114	57	438	44,100.250	2,203.65
1879	St. Kilda	207	80	46	333	23,116.850	2,350.00
1884	Silhet	298	131	108	537	115,387.565	9,218.00
1886	British Peer	331	136	156	623	78,663.425	8,900.00
1887	John Davis	290	98	92	480	37,908.015	10,333.00
1889	Jumna I	237	142	148	587	95,126.345	20,045.00
1890	Jumna II	333	116	121	570	71,675.180	10,746.00
1891	British Peer	360	122	119	601	86,034.095	16,563.00
1895	Grecian	339	142	124	605	89,687.880	15,501.35
1897	Foyle	131	49	33	213	26,837.370	3,697.60
1898	Arno	434	157	152	743	91,588.720	14,750.00
1900	Earne	142	49	38	229	40,600.300	5,572.25
1903	Rhone	236	50	32	318	48,245.540	5,099.00
1905	Avon	485	134	115	734	80,084.710	11,433.50
1907	SS Mutlah	182	29	20	231	33,311.000	4,322.50
1909	SS Mutlah	371	76	54	501	38,700.525	4,026.50
1911	SS Sutlej	418	105	80	603	57,995.860	10,800.00

Source: British Parliamentary Papers, *Report on the Condition of Indian Immigrants in Four British Colonies (Trinidad, British Guiana or Demerara, Jamaica and Fiji) and in the Dutch Colony of Suriname or Dutch Guiana (McNeill-Lal Report)*, vol. 47, part 2 (Cd. 7744) (London: HMSO, 1915), 180 of appendix 21.

Despite low wages, Indians were able to remit as well as deposit savings in each Caribbean colony. In 1908, 832 and 726 former indentured Indians from British Guiana and Trinidad took with them 118,365 and 280,716 rupees, respectively, to India. The average for British Guiana was 142 rupees while it was 386 for Trinidad (British Guiana 1909, 1–4). Table 11 shows how much

TABLE 12: FORMER INDENTURED LABORERS' INDIVIDUAL SAVINGS					
Year	Name	Gender	Occupation	Plantation	Amount
1869	Beharry	Male	Shovelman	Peter's Hall	$600
1890	Badlu	Male	Barber	Blairmont	$420
1891	Debaran	Male	Shovelman	Albion	$300
1891	Jhakri	Male	Weeder	No. 59 Village	$250
1891	Pargasia	Female	Weeder	Rimveldt	$360
1892	Ramkali	Female	Weeder	Albion	$225
1893	Jasoda	Female	Weeder	Albouystown	$750
1893	Rampersad	Male	Driver	Pouderoyen	$1,100
1895	Gonesh	Male	Shovelman	Bath	$209
1895	Kaino Sing	Male	Shovelman	Enmore	$220
1895	Ramdari	Male	Weeder	Albion	$300
1895	Dheunki	Male	Shovelman	Albion	$310
1895	Shewbahadur	Male	Shovelman	Bath	$400
1895	Debidin	Male	Goldsmith	Port Mourant	$420

Source: British Guiana, "Report of the Immigration Agent General for the Year 1906–1907," in *The Argosy* (Georgetown, Guyana: Demerara, 1908).

money and jewelry was deposited from 1878 to 1911 in Suriname by return-ing immigrants for payment to them on arrival in India. These figures are in florins: one florin equals one shilling and eight pence or one rupee and four annas.

While tables 10 and 11 provide an example of the overall savings among Indian laborers, table 12 shows the individual savings earned by some labor-ers for selected years. These individual savings are generally lost in the larger picture of indenture and remittances among indentured Indians. Table 12 shows the highest sums of money remitted by indentured Indians from British Guiana for the selected years of 1869–95.

Certain analyses can be drawn from these statistics on savings. If the value of gold jewelry—which Indians took with them in person—were included, the figures would be much higher. On almost every return ship, Indians, particularly women, had gold jewelry and other trinkets on them. Some of the women possessed a good deal in the shape of coins fastened together for necklaces, nose rings, and bangles on their wrists and feet (Brit-ish Parliamentary Papers 1871, 33). From 1854 to 1890, jewelry taken back from British Guiana to India was valued at $280,000 (Comins 1893a, 45). However, in some colonies returnees took back their savings in person, which were not declared to the immigration officials. The reason for not declaring their savings to colonial officials was partly related to their traditional village customs and the mistrust of Western financial institutions. As in rural India, some traditional Indians never believed in depositing their money in banks, fearing that they wouldn't be able to withdraw it at their convenience. Whenever they deposited their savings in Western banks, they would simply withdraw some of their money to make sure it was still there. During indenture, and even now, Indians would stash their money under mattresses, in the ground, and in the holes of trees. They would also pretend not to have any savings to discourage relatives from asking for financial help. Therefore, the statistics do not reveal the exact amount of savings taken back from the Caribbean to India. The statistics are also based on the average of the returnees' savings, a number that often included children, who had no savings. Some returnees took as much as $1,000 with them. One individual, besides the sum he remitted through the government, took with him a bill of exchange on the bank of Calcutta for $2,000 (British Parliamentary Papers 1866, 24).

The figures in table 12 represent the glowing picture the planters pointed to in their continued effort to promote migration from India. The reality was that few indentured servants, if any, could have earned that much money from indenture or by themselves. If a laborer was earning twenty-four cents per day for 280 days per year, the maximum he could have earned from five years of indentured service in the Caribbean was $336. An indentured woman would have earned far less since women were paid ten cents per day. The substantial savings some returnees took back were from earnings of the entire family and from other occupations (trading, shop keeping, and money lending) not directly related to indentured service. For example, in 1895 on Plantation Port Mourant, the indentured Debidin remitted $420 to India, but his occupation was listed as goldsmith. Of the returnees, less than half took back with them an average of about forty to fifty pounds, or $300 to $500.

By contrast, the spectacular savings recorded provide a misleading picture of the indenture system. Many returnees went back with nothing but the clothes on their backs. Table 13 demonstrates the hidden side of indenture. On every return ship from the Caribbean were those of unsound mind. They were not allowed to return to their homeland until they had received treatment and waited for one year before being determined fit to travel. Yet many with unsound minds or marginally unsound minds made it onboard the return ships because of loopholes in the repatriation system.

TABLE 13: NUMBER AND PERCENTAGE OF RETURNEES WITHOUT SAVINGS, 1907–10			
Year	No. returnees	No. without savings	Percent without savings
1907	4,212	1,495	35.49
1908	4,197	1,560	37.16
1909	3,941	1,597	22.00
1910	2,727	1,410	51.70

Source: *Report on Emigration from the Port of Calcutta to British and Foreign Colonies* for the years 1907–10 (Calcutta: Bengal Secretariat Press, 1908; 1909; 1910; 1911).

Moreover, the registration of the savings was poorly conducted. Sometimes savings of one indentured Indian appeared under another person's name, causing much confusion. Worst of all, the savings sometimes never reached heirs in India because relatives had migrated or died or colonial authorities had misspelled the names of indentured Indians and relatives during the registration process, which made it difficult to trace heirs.

RETURN SEA VOYAGE

One of the main problems with the return voyage from the Caribbean was the irregular schedule. Ships did not arrive on time to take returnees home. Considerable time lapsed in nearly all colonies before returnees were sent to India. Some returnees became so frustrated with waiting that they simply abandoned the idea of returning home and re-indentured themselves to five and even ten years in the Caribbean. Apart from ships arriving late, the colonial authorities claimed that the returnees did not follow the procedure for returning home. Many would not register as required but showed up at ports when the return ships arrived. Likewise, many returnees would register to return to India but changed their minds when the ships arrived. To deal with this problem, the colonial authorities waited until the registration was overbooked. If they wanted five hundred returnees, they would wait until fifteen hundred signed up to return to India, which explains the late arrival of ships.

Ships generally left in August or September to avoid distractions from plantation work routine and the winter voyage around the Cape of Good Hope (Laurence 1994, 363). The arrangement of returning Indians was straightforward but not without inconveniences. Returnees were required to register ahead of time with an immigration office for ships to be chartered. Ships left from the colonies at least once a year. Returnees were quite

aware of the procedures for returning home; many learned from those who
had gone to India and returned. Others, through the painful procedure of
waiting long periods before departure, inadvertently had ample time to
process their credentials. The procedure before departure was as follows:
remittances were checked, passage money was paid, money deposited was
certified, and medical and clothing inspections were carried out (Ramesar
1994). The crew of the outward (from India) as well as the inward (to India)
voyage consisted of a surgeon who was previously employed in the service
of transporting people on the high seas, a staff of assistants consisting of
individuals who were compounders and interpreters, a *topaz* for each one
hundred adults, two professional cooks, and, in the later stages, an Indian
immigration officer from the colonies. Nonetheless, diseases and deaths were
a common feature on the arriving and departing voyages. Some common
diseases on the departing voyage were cholera, typhoid, dysentery, scurvy,
malaria, leprosy, and scorbutic diarrhea. These diseases caused a number of
deaths on return ships from the Caribbean to India. For example, in 1905,
2,775, 787, and 650 Indians left Demerara, Trinidad, and Jamaica, respectively,
and the deaths numbered fifty-three, fourteen, and fourteen, an average of
1.90 percent, 1.78 percent, and 2.05 percent, respectively (British Guiana
1907, 13). The large number of aged people, chronic invalids, and persons in
a poor state of health were factors given for the mortality rate on the return
ships. However, by the 1890s, the death rates on both arriving and departing ships were much lower, largely due to improved facilities as well as the
laborers' familiarity with the sea voyage. Those in the Caribbean would not
risk returning if they felt they were unfit mentally and physically to endure
the long sea journey.

The mindset of the returnees was different from that of the arrivals. To
recall, except for the second-time migrants, the arrivals were not familiar
with the entire indenture system, from the time of recruitment to the sea
voyage to the plantations. They became familiar with the indenture system
with their own firsthand experience, and each stage held great uncertainties.
For example, many had not experienced life outside of their villages, much
less a distant environment such as the Caribbean with a rigid race and
class system. Nor were they exposed to any other major religions beyond
Hinduism and Islam. The voyage experience for most arrivals was one of
ambivalence, and, therefore, makeshift alliances across different castes and
religions were formed to survive. The sea voyage experience of the returnees
was somewhat different. They knew what to expect on the ships as well as
upon landing in their homeland. However, the mood was not all joyous.

There were those who were returning home empty-handed after spending at least five years away from their villages. They must have asked themselves what went wrong. Why were they unable to acquire any savings? Their experience in the Caribbean was one of basic survival. The colonial authorities ascribed their poverty to their own idleness, extravagance, illness, and improvidence. There was also a third of the number among the returnees who had unsound minds and various illnesses. To these individuals the return journey was obviously not a happy one and was perhaps worse than when they first left India. When they left India, they had dreams, but now their dreams had been dashed. Relationships—marriage across caste and religion—formed out of desperation to deal with the pressures of plantation life that had boded well during indenture were suddenly jeopardized. One high-caste woman who had married a low-caste man in the Caribbean and lived with him for ten years said to him upon their return to India, "you low-caste man; I will have nothing more to do with you" (British Parliamentary Paper 1910b, 94). Some returnees abandoned their families. Some Indians who were converted to Christianity were waving the Bible before reaching India. Just before their arrival in India, there was much expectant excitement—shoving, singing, and dancing—for many people had not seen their homeland in about twenty to thirty years.

The returnees followed a planned procedure. When they arrived and passed through the depot, they were taken to the banks to cash their checks and then dispatched by railroad to their specific destinations. Some stayed in and around the city where they disembarked. The destitute were given a small sum of money—about ten to twenty-five rupees—to fend for themselves. Some of the returnees did not exit the depot but asked to be re-indentured to their former indentured colony or to another one. Special arrangements were made for them, mainly placing them away from new intending emigrants. These returnees were eventually dispatched the following year to a colony of their choice. Other returnees joined the crowded and squalid surroundings of the inner city—malaria-ridden, without work, nourishment, or medical relief.

READJUSTMENT AND REMIGRATION

To understand the readjustment challenges returnees faced in India, it is instructive to examine the Indian social structure in India and then in the Caribbean. Indians were stratified according to the enclosed caste system.

The main characteristics of the caste system were ascription at birth according to skin color or parental religion, the insistence on endogamy, and the recognition and guarding against ritual pollution, essentially the restriction of contact between members of different castes. The Indian social structure revolved and functioned on strict caste rules. Migration from families and villages and especially over water was a violation of caste rules, and most often caste violators were ostracized. Those Indians who were brought to the Caribbean were perceived by their village to have broken caste and were treated as outsiders. In the Caribbean, the Indian caste system experienced transformation and virtually disappeared, mainly because of a Western-oriented plantation work routine that did not recognize or revolve around caste rules based on purity and rank. The Christian missionary efforts—especially among the Presbyterians—aimed at converting Indians from Hinduism to Christianity; shortages of women; the long distance between India and the Caribbean; the cultural differences between the East and West; the immigrant diversity with regard to religion, geography, language, and economic opportunities; and immigrant initiatives to get rid of the stern social structure contributed to the overall breakdown of the caste system. This dual experience of leaving India with a social stigma and the breakdown of their caste structure in the Caribbean placed those who were returning in a rather precarious situation. The question they might have asked themselves is how would they be accepted in their former homeland with their new overseas experience that was essentially different from what it was when they first entered the Caribbean? How much of their new experiences, which were not all bad, were they willing to dismiss to be integrated back into their villages? The returnees had to first adjust to the Caribbean, and upon returning to India they had to adjust for the second time, although they were returning to a society with which they were more familiar. Whatever they chose to be or do, their villages' view of them remained static. Their overseas experience had transformed them into strangers in their own land of birth. Mahatma Gandhi commented that these people were social lepers who did not even know the language of the people.

> They all looked famished. Their lot is the lowest ebb of human misery. The fact that the majority of these men are Colonial born aggravates their misery . . . These men are neither Indian nor Colonial. They have no Indian culture in the foreign land they go to, save what they picked up from their uncultured half-dis-Indianised parents. They are Colonial in that they are debarred access to the Colonial, i.e., Western

Culture. They are therefore out of the frying pan into the fire. There, at least they had some money and a kind of a home. Here they are social lepers, not even knowing the language of the people (Sannyasi and Chaturvedi 1931, 9).

While the state of some of the returnees was dismal, and indeed a small percentage of them were disease-ridden and insane before leaving India and their situation worsened during indenture in the Caribbean, Gandhi's views of the returnees were an overstatement and overreaction. Indians were returning to a familiar environment, and even if they were away for five years, it would not have been that much of a challenge to readjust to the system that they were born and raised into until they were adults. Moreover, they were making accommodated shifts to indenture in the Caribbean until the time was ready for them to return home. Indians who had planned to return home never really relinquished their homeland identity. But certainly Caribbean Indian–born children would have encountered problems of adjustment to a social caste system that they did not know or understand. Caribbean Indian–born children generally chafed at the caste-driven social structure around them in India. Their Caribbean experience instilled a new or an alternative sense of identity (class) among them, one that was inconsistent with the social customs and expectations of village life in India. In spite of this difference, there was a steady stream of returnees from the Caribbean. For example, 5,580 colonial or Caribbean-born children were taken by their parents to India from British Guiana from 1871 to 1890 (Comins 1893a, 46). These children would have certainly encountered challenges of social adjustment in an environment where caste rules were firmly entrenched. Some Indians in Suriname did not go back to India precisely because of their Caribbean-born children (British Parliamentary Papers 1915, 168). To have Indians stay in the Caribbean instead of sending them back to India, the colonial authorities argued that the returning children were at a major disadvantage in learning new customs and ways (Comins 1893b, 9). However, it is important to stress that the caste and class systems were not that extreme in structure and function. Caribbean Indians were not living in a fluid class system, and in particular, they were stratified or relegated to the basement or the lowest rung of the Caribbean social structure. Indians entered into another social class structure that revolved around racial characteristics, which placed them at the lowest level. But there were differences. The long-term residents, in particular those who spent at least ten years in the Caribbean, faced adjustment challenges in their homelands.

For example, from 1871 to 1890, one in 125 returnees spent anywhere from twenty-two to forty-four years in British Guiana (Comins 1893a, 46). Living and working in the Caribbean with little meaningful contact with their home-based environment and where there were, at least in theory, no caste rules or where the customs and cultures were different from those to which they were accustomed would have certainly caused some basic changes in their mannerisms, speech, and culinary habits. Some former indentured laborers indeed acquired a taste for rum, meat, and fish in their sojourn in the Caribbean and therefore violated caste rules (Samaroo 1982, 45–72). Ironically, they were inadvertently exposed to a different social structure that brought some benefits to the disadvantaged and deprived. Low-caste Indians, for the most part, gained from the indenture system mainly because, as stated earlier, the caste rules on the Caribbean sugar plantations were reversed (Roopnarine 2007, 70). Arguably, the low caste would resist an environment where the important positions and work experience they had acquired were not recognized. The returnees did not only look different in dress and appearance but they also behaved differently. Oliver Warner, a colonial official, noticed a marked difference between an Indian leaving India and a returning Indian. He said when an Indian arrived in the Caribbean he or she would normally stoop to the feet of authority figures, but when an Indian left the Caribbean, he or she would say "How do you do, Sir?" (British Parliamentary Papers 1910b, 29–30).

There was an option or opportunity for returning Indians to reintegrate into their castes. But there were implications. A returnee could reclaim his or her caste status through a purification ceremony. The ceremony was very expensive, mainly because the returnees had to give up a substantial amount of their savings to provide feasts for the priests and other respected members of the village. An immigration report in 1881 stated, "return immigrants frequently dissipate the bulk of their savings shortly after in India, feeding their 'Gurus' (Spiritual advisers) and feasting their friends. Relatives innumerable, with the most remote claims to kinship appear when least expected, on the arrival of a well-to-do Indian in his native 'bustee' (village) and hard earned savings are soon squandered in vain oblations to the family penates and 'barra khanas' to his kindred" (British Guiana 1882, 5). While an unknown number of returnees chose to be reinstated into their caste, some of them did not return to their villages, instead choosing to stay around the depot waiting to return to the Caribbean or migrate to the urban sprawl of Calcutta mainly to conceal that they had gone to the Caribbean. They refused to go along with the caste purification ceremony. They stayed away from

TABLE 14: INDENTURED INDIANS WHO REMIGRATED TO THE SAME OR
ANOTHER COLONY, 1908–11

Year	No. who remigrated
1908	383
1909	316
1910	478
1911	475

Source: *Report on Emigration from the Port of Calcutta to British and Foreign Colonies* for the years 1908–12 (Calcutta: Bengal Secretariat Press, 1909; 1910; 1911; 1912).

TABLE 15: NUMBER AND PERCENTAGE OF INDENTURED INDIANS WHO
RE-INDENTURED FROM INDIA, 1908–11

Colony departed	No. who re-indentured	Percent
Demerara	22	5.74
Fiji	148	38.64
Jamaica	27	7.06
Natal	51	13.31
Suriname	39	10.18
Trinidad	96	25.06

Source: *Report on Emigration from the Port of Calcutta to British and Foreign Colonies* for the years 1908–12 (Calcutta: Bengal Secretariat Press, 1909; 1910; 1911; 1912; 1913).

their villages to avoid caste exclusion and family members who wanted to swindle them out of their savings. Other returnees changed or terminated their Caribbean relationships.

There is very limited information on what actually happened to those returnees who went back to their villages. There is information, however, on those who returned to India and were willing or waiting to go back to the Caribbean for the second time. Although these second-time migrants were considerably smaller in number compared to the first-time migrants, their migration for the second time to the Caribbean poses a serious challenge to neoslave scholarship or literature of indenture. Why would these migrants want to return to the Caribbean as indentured laborers when indenture was described and defined as "a new system of slavery"? To illustrate, table 14 shows that from 1908 to 1911 an estimated 1,652 Indians returned to the Caribbean for the second time. Table 15 shows the percentage of those who returned from the Caribbean and decided to go back for a second time. In one instance, an estimated 38 percent decided to go back to an indentured colony for the second time.

If we use a conservative estimate that about four hundred Indians migrated for a second time in a period of eighty years, then about thirty-two thousand of them who served indenture in the Caribbean returned to India and then back to the Caribbean. Actually, about fifty thousand Indians went back to the Caribbean as indentured servants for a second and even third time (Roopnarine 2009c, 88). Some paid their own passage and therefore were not recorded. The remigration to the Caribbean would have been much higher had not the authorities placed strict immigration regulations on second-term emigrants. Even when some intending returnees were rejected, they hung around the depots hoping they would somehow make it through the immigration gates to the Caribbean. Why would thousands want to go back to the Caribbean and work under slave-like conditions? Was it that India was worse than the Caribbean? It is an important question that is beyond the scope of this chapter but deserves analysis elsewhere.

Chapter Four

INDIAN MIGRATION WITHIN THE CARIBBEAN

The previous chapters examined Indian migration during the period of indenture, namely from India to the Caribbean, within the Caribbean, and back to India between 1838 and 1920, although some analyses on return migration from the Caribbean until 1955 were presented. The following chapters move on from the indenture period and assess Indian migration after indentured emancipation from 1920 to the modern period. This chapter on Indian intra-Caribbean migration analyzes the movement of Indians from one Caribbean territory to the next, starting with the movement of the Indo-Guyanese from their homeland to Suriname, Trinidad, and Barbados. The focus is then shifted to the movement of Indo-Trinidadians and Indo-Lucians to the US Virgin Islands. While some attention is paid to the Indian intraregional migration from 1920 to 1960, the main focus will be from 1960 to the modern period, mainly to coincide with major migration patterns during this migration phase. The Indo-Guyanese will be given more attention because they have been the most active intraregional migrants in the Caribbean.

INDO-GUYANESE MIGRATION TO SURINAME

There are some characteristics of Indo-Guyanese migration that set it apart from other forms of Indian intraregional migration. The movement of Indo-Guyanese within the Caribbean has been essentially a movement from an underdeveloped Guyana to semideveloped countries in the Caribbean. Guyana is ranked the second-poorest country in the Caribbean, after Haiti. Any movement out of Guyana naturally implies that migration would be to another country that is doing better, however marginally. The movement of Indo-Guyanese has undoubtedly created a secondary diaspora that, in some ways, parallels the primary extra-regional diaspora in Queens, New York, (Little Guyana) in scope and intensity. For instance, the movement of Indo-Guyanese within the Caribbean is more regular and problem-oriented than the movement of Indo-Guyanese to New York and elsewhere. The reason for this is that intraregional migration tends to create social and economic pressure that leads to regional instability. Most of the countries in the Caribbean are found in the developing zone and therefore do not have the resources to accommodate the influx of immigrants. Guyana, Grenada, and St. Vincent are the major sending countries, while Trinidad, Barbados, and the US Virgin Islands are the major receiving countries/islands in the intraregional migration circuit. Comparative analyses are rare between the two diasporas. Certainly, the lack of scholarly attention has led to a poor understanding of Indo-Guyanese intraregional migration. It is often believed that migration and interaction among Caribbean nationals are fluid, at least when compared to the larger movement to Europe and North America. While this may be true because of the close historical ties and location, the Caribbean islands are better positioned to understand the roots of conflict, but some questions are warranted. Do Caribbean nationals or ethnic groups like Indians face challenges of acceptance when migrating and settling within a Caribbean that is similar in ethnicity? Do Caribbean nationals face problems of assimilation when migrating within the Caribbean despite similar historical and cultural backgrounds? Does the regional background or ethnicity of the migrants often lead to marginalization and discrimination in the intraregional migration circuit? Does migration within the Caribbean, irrespective of class, gender, ethnicity, or region, provide opportunities for identity to be contested and reconstructed into new mores? This chapter explores these themes.

Indo-Guyanese migration to Suriname can be divided into two time periods: 1920–60 and 1960–2015. The first phase was an intraregional colonial migration since Guyana and Suriname were still under British and Dutch rule, respectively. The movement was small and temporary in nature, although some migrants stayed in the receiving destinations. The movement was not one-way from Guyana to Suriname but moved also from Suriname to Guyana. This movement was not all dependent on opportunities in the receiving destinations. Instead, migration was dictated by global events such as the impact of the Great Depression and civil unrest in the Caribbean in the first quarter of the twentieth century. This intraregional colonial migration was determined by the initiatives and efforts from Indian religious organizations and aspirations from individual Indian migrants. Soon after indentured emancipation, Indians started to stake claims to opportunities beyond their insular plantation domains. They began to actively seek employment opportunities in urban areas as well as other Caribbean territories. This aspiration coincided with works of various Christian denominations that provided Indians with the training and skills needed to become qualified for jobs beyond the plantation system. Even those who were not interested in Christian-influenced forms of training were concerned about the stagnation of early postindenture plantation life and began to migrate from this environment when possible. Given the close proximity of Suriname to the county of Berbice, in Guyana, with a majority Indian population, it was natural that Indians would migrate to Suriname not only for economic but also for cultural reasons. New Nickerie, a major town on the banks of the Corentyne River in Suriname, has been home to a sizable postindentured influx of Indians. Ethnographic research reveals that an unknown number of Indians have migrated from Guyana to Suriname and settled, marrying Indo-Surinamese. Likewise, an unknown number of Indo-Surinamese migrated and settled in Guyana, marrying Indo-Guyanese. Some Indo-Surinamese have actually migrated from the distant capital city of Paramaribo to New Nickerie and then to Guyana looking for Indian spouses. In one village, near the town of Skeldon in Guyana, there are some descendants from the early migration. They are known individually as "Dutchman" or "Dutchboy." These descendants do visit their former homeland, but they are generally more Guyanese than Indo-Surinamese.[1]

This early phase of postindenture migration from Guyana to Suriname was always small but regular, which prevented the formation of an Indo-Guyanese community in Suriname or the formation of an Indo-Surinamese community in Guyana. The migrants were scattered in urban areas and in the coastal agricultural belt. They were difficult to detect since they blended seamlessly into the Indian community from the same ethnic background. These migrants were practically absorbed into their new communities despite efforts to retain some of their culture, such as the Hindustani language among the Indo-Surinamese migrants in Guyana. The size of this early migration is not precisely known, but it is safe to say that it comprised around five thousand to eight thousand migrants between 1920 and 1960. This migration was driven more by cultural rather than economic reasons. Both Suriname and Guyana were underdeveloped colonies reeling from the effects of colonialism, which stymied economic opportunities and endeavors such as investment in small business. Language differences between the countries (Dutch in Suriname and English in Guyana) also restricted migration between the two countries, especially with regard to skill employment. However, the main reason for the early migration between the two countries was cultural, to reestablish Indian cultural relations—Hindu and Muslim—as well as intermarriage through Santan Dharma and Arya Samaj religious associations. In spite of the breakdown of some aspects of their social structure, such as caste, in their new environment, Indians still expressed preference to marry within their own ethnic group. When this was not possible within their immediate village system, they would migrate on either side of the Corentyne River between Guyana and Suriname to look for spouses. One elderly Guyanese woman noted that "plenty Guyanese married Surinamese people and stayed in Suriname."[2]

INDO-GUYANESE MIGRATION TO SURINAME, 1960–2015

The modern period of migration (1960–2015) between Suriname and Guyana was much larger than the early phase of migration. It is a migration that began when the two former colonies achieved independence: Guyana in 1966 and Suriname in 1975. The two independent nations, especially following the first decade of independence, were trapped in the neocolonial world of development and shaken by domestic political turmoil and ethnic tensions. These events generated a wave of movement in and out of these countries. Guyana was quickly suffocated with the introduction of cooperative socialism through systemic discrimination, marginalization, and militarization, which transformed the country into one of the poorest in the Caribbean (Singh 1988). The return of a semifree government under the predominantly Indian-led politicians brought some relief to the country, but economic hardships, stagnant quality of life, crime, corruption, and racial and ethnic tensions taxed and tested the will of the Guyanese to remain at home. Many sought whatever means possible to escape from Guyana. One fifty-year-old interviewee in No. 72 Village, Corentyne, said, "I went to Suriname because of no work in my village and the cost of living was high. The Guyana money does not have much value. I had some experience with bakery, actually they call me Baker, and so when I went Suriname I was able to find a job as a baker." When asked why he returned to Guyana, he said he had saved some money and wanted to use the money to build his own house and be self-employed. But more importantly, he wanted "his children to grow up like a Guyanese and go to school in Guyana." The dozen or so male interviewees in the same village who migrated to Suriname in the 1970s and 1980s shared basically the same reasons for leaving Guyana: to search for work, to "make life" better, to receive a favorable exchange rate from saving Surinamese currency, and the hope to return and settle down in Guyana.[3]

In Suriname, Indo-Guyanese migration was propelled by pull factors. When Suriname became independent in 1975, Surinamese were given the option to stay or migrate to Holland, the former mother country. The option was for five years. Between 1975 and 1980, an estimated half of the population of Suriname migrated to the Netherlands, a majority of them Hindustani. The latter migrants feared living under the newly postindependence Creole government. The domestic situation worsened when the military toppled the civilian government in 1980, unleashing a wave of terror in the country. The international community, including the Netherlands and the United States, withdrew aid and placed trade restrictions on the country, plunging Suriname into an economic downward spiral (see Choenni 2013). The migration of Surinamese individuals to the Netherlands, however, created a labor vacuum, especially in the rice, banana, and sugar industries, which was filled by Indo-Guyanese migrants. One interviewee at the open market in New Nickerie in Suriname had this to say about Indo-Guyanese migration to Suriname:

I am an Indian Guyanese woman who is forty years old, and I migrated to Suriname about twenty years ago because my mother migrated first. When I came here things were really hard for me and other Guyanese. We Guyanese do not speak Dutch and we have no Dutch education, which is needed to get a good job. If you want a Dutch education you have to go to school, but we are too old to do that. You have to go to when you are small. So we Guyanese work in banana industry as day laborers and buy and sell in the marketplace.[4]

Another interviewee in the same market revealed the following:

I am an Indo-Surinamese woman who speaks Dutch, Hindi, English, and Takie-Takie, and my husband is an Indo-Guyanese who came to Suriname when he was three years old. My husband's mother used to live in Suriname, but she went back to Guyana but comes back and visits us. Hardship brought Guyanese to Suriname and some never go back. My husband is a fisherman and he has four Guyanese working for him catching fish and four Guyanese working for him on his farm. They are all hard working, but they smoke dope.[5]

An Indian female Suriname vendor, selling mainly Indian CDs, said she is half-Guyanese and half-Surinamese since her father came from Guyana and met her mother in Suriname in the 1970s. The above views demonstrate how complex the Indo-Guyanese migration has been. There are many types of Indo-Guyanese in Suriname: (1) there are those who migrated and settled and married other Guyanese; (2) there are those who migrated and married Surinamese and formed hybrid families; (3) there are those who travel regularly between Guyana and Suriname and are staying in Suriname on a short-term basis. Some Indo-Guyanese have also married Creole Surinamese.

The Indo-Guyanese population in Suriname is currently (2015) about twenty thousand, and an estimated four thousand to six thousand reside in New Nickerie and the surrounding agricultural belt. During the 1970s and 1980s, there were over forty thousand Indo-Guyanese in Suriname working or conducting legal and illegal trade. A majority of Indo-Guyanese were found in low-level, unskilled jobs like those in the rice and banana industries and were mainly satisfied with their transplanted life situation because the standard of living and security in Guyana was worse. However, by the end of the 1980s and the early 1990s many were forced to return home. Conditions in Suriname deteriorated because of a civil war, while the political and economic situation in Guyana improved marginally because of a new government. These events coupled with the devaluation of the Surinamese guilder caused, ironically, a small but continuous stream of Indo-Surinamese to join in with the return migration of Guyanese to their homeland. Suriname has since recovered, and in the first decade of the twenty-first century has moved toward technological methods of cultivating rice and thereby further reduced the need for manual unskilled labor in the rice industry. However, the banana industry at Lakatan still employs Indo-Guyanese workers on a seasonal basis through work permits, contributing to modest but continuous migration of Indo-Guyanese laborers to Suriname.

INDO-GUYANESE IN SURINAME

How are Indo-Guyanese treated in Suriname, and, in particular, by the Indo-Surinamese? Soon after indentured emancipation in 1920, Indo-Guyanese were well received in Suriname, primarily because of the urge to establish cultural ties relating to India as well as to their shared experience as former indentured servants. This good cultural relation continued into the 1970s, when Indo-Guyanese were appreciated for their dedication to hard manual labor in agricultural fields. By the 1980s, relations between the two groups took an ominous turn. Indo-Guyanese were singled out and blamed for rising crime and pressure on social services in Suriname. The Surinamese government was caught in a quandary; that is, it needed the cheap supply of labor to boost the economy but was worried about the impact of these migrants on Suriname's society. During the 1980s, under the leadership of Dési Bouterse, Guyanese migrants were immediately rounded up and repatriated back to Guyana. The real reason for the repatriation was that Suriname was in a steady economic decline and did not have the resources to accommodate foreigners. Most Caribbean countries are unprepared to integrate foreigners into their own country. The perception that Guyanese migrants were a burden to Suriname has had an indelible impact on the relations between the two similar ethnic groups. Guyanese migrants have been criticized for any infractions in Suriname. One Guyanese migrant who has lived in Suriname for over two decades declared, "to a Dutchman, Guyanese are low-class people and the women are whores. Why? Because of the hardship Guyanese experienced during the Burnham years, when they came to Suriname. They had to hustle and many women turned to prostitution."[6]

There is some merit to this assessment of the Guyanese in Suriname. Many came from low socioeconomic backgrounds and some were already engaged in low-skilled jobs and other questionable occupations before they went to Suriname. Some men were fleeing from the law in Guyana and were reentering a life of crime in Suriname. In 1979, a Surinamese couple was brutally murdered in their home in New Nickerie, and the police immediately rounded up Guyanese individuals for questioning, in the process violating basic human rights standards. The reckless roundup was based on the perception that Guyanese are crime prone. Women who were already prostitutes in Guyana continued this profession in Suriname. They were aware that most Guyanese men who went to Suriname were single and capitalized on meeting their sexual needs. Whatever might have been the reasons for Guyanese being in Suriname, the perception, according to one Guyanese taxi driver who has lived in Suriname for over thirty years, is that "once you are a Guyanese in Suriname you will remain a Guyanese. Surinamese tolerate but do not accept Guyanese."[7]

INDO-GUYANESE MIGRATION TO TRINIDAD AND BARBADOS

The movement of Indo-Guyanese to Trinidad and Barbados shares similar features to the movement to Suriname. Indo-Guyanese migrate to these islands because of geographical closeness, common history, culture, language, family networks in the receiving destinations, and favorable immigration laws for skilled workers like nurses, teachers, and doctors. There are some differences, however. Upon achieving independence in the 1960s, Guyana, Trinidad, and Barbados created their own natural border and developed their own idea of citizenship, which essentially reduced the freedom of movement given to colonial people within the British Empire. A visa and other requirements were needed to travel between former colonies of the same empire. This new development with regard to the movement of Caribbean people within the Caribbean was not welcome by some countries with struggling economies. Subsequently, a free movement clause within the Caribbean Community (CARICOM) called CARICOM Single Market and Economy (CSME) allowed for skilled persons to be granted the right to move and work freely throughout the Caribbean region. Indo-Guyanese took advantage of this liberal immigration clause and migrated to Trinidad and Barbados. This movement was dictated and determined by the national government rather than precipitated by the migrants themselves. Unskilled persons were not given the same free movement as skilled persons. Indo-Guyanese migration to Trinidad and Barbados was also dictated by personal reasons. Economic deprivation was one main factor that pushed them out of Guyana, a country affected by political and ethnic tensions as well as poor economic performance. This outward migration has generally been dictated by the desire to join communities of similar ethnic composition and tradition. Some Indo-Guyanese migrated to Trinidad because the large Indian population in that country makes it feel like home, while other migrants or younger ones have followed the pattern of their relatives and parents and migrate with them or at a later time on an individual basis.

The Indo-Guyanese migration to Barbados has not been dictated by ties of ethnicity but by economic factors. Like Trinidad, Barbados has a higher human development status and has experienced economic growth, especially in tourism-related activities and direct foreign investment. Barbados's per capita income is the highest in the Eastern Caribbean region at $17,300 and ranks high in the United Nations Development Program's Human Development Index at 38 out of 183. In contrast, Guyana's per capita income is around $3,000. The world migration pattern has shown that migrants go

TABLE 16: DECLINING POPULATION RATES OF AFRICANS AND INDIANS IN GUYANA, 1980–2002

Ethnic Group	1980	1991	2002
Africans	234,094	233,468	226,861
Indians	394,417	351,939	326,395

Source: 2002 Guyana Census, www.statisticsguyana.gov.gy/census.html.

to a country with a higher level of human development than their country of origin.[8] The migration pattern between Guyana and Barbados is no exception. Development in Barbados has created job opportunities, which in turn has attracted working-class Guyanese laborers. Additionally, a job vacuum has emerged in Barbados, mainly because Barbadians have moved to proverbially greener pastures like Europe and North America, and those who have remained in the country do not want to participate in low-paid menial employment. Working-class Guyanese laborers accept these positions.

The lack of solid demographic information on ethnicity makes the Indo-Guyanese population in Trinidad and Barbados a matter of speculation. Like elsewhere in the world, Caribbean countries do not compile immigration data based on ethnicity. The *Trinidad Express* newspaper reported that there are over twenty-five thousand illegal Guyanese migrants in Trinidad and Tobago. Estimated figures of Guyanese migrants in Barbados vary from thirty thousand to forty thousand. It is safe to say that about 70 percent of Guyanese migrants in Trinidad and Barbados are of Indian extraction. The rationale for this conclusion is that more Indians than African Guyanese have left Guyana since the 1980s, as indicated in table 16. While negative growth rates between the two major ethnic groups may be related to higher deaths and lower births, the major cause is outward migration.

The Indian population declined from 51.1 percent in 1980 to 48.6 percent in 1991 to 43.5 percent in 2002, an estimated reduction of about seventy thousand, whereas the African population decreased by ten thousand for the same period in Guyana. By contrast, the Indian population from 1970 to 1990 in Trinidad and Suriname increased from 40.0 to 40.3 percent and from 30.0 to 37.0 percent, respectively (Garcia 2004, 410). The challenge still remains as to where these Indian migrants went. More is known about the outward migration of Indo-Guyanese individuals to Queens, New York, but less about the intraregional migration. While it is possible that more than 50 percent went to New York and other destinations in Europe and North America, it is safe to say that at least 30 percent went to other regions in the Caribbean. That would place the Indo-Guyanese population in Trinidad and

Barbados around forty thousand. More information is available as to what has happened to the Indo-Guyanese population in Trinidad and Barbados: (1) their migration to these destinations continues, although not in large numbers; (2) they are either long- or short-term residents; (3) more than half of them do not have legal rights; and (4) they have not formed a distinct minority or a distinct community, although this may happen in the future.

INDO-GUYANESE IN TRINIDAD

There isn't any established recognizable Indo-Guyanese community in Trinidad like the one in Queens, New York, mainly because in Trinidad they are first-generation migrants who are in the process of establishing a community. However, when Indo-Guyanese migrants enter Trinidad, they prefer to reside in Chaguanas, San Juan, El Socorro, and Aranguez, where the percentage of Indo-Trinidadians is higher. The decision is based on the perception that their adjustment and needs (housing, employment, protection, trust) in their new society would be less challenging in these areas. Even if these expectations are not realized, the consequence of such desire is that their day-to-day lives are different from Indians who migrated and settled in non-Indian enclaves. There is not a deep desire to build a new community but rather to blend in and integrate themselves like they had done before leaving their adopted Guyanese homeland. There is not an urge to create a segmented community like other Indians in Queens, New York, because of racism and marginalization. These intraregional migrants generally enter into a community in Trinidad that is ethnologically similar to the one they left behind in Guyana. Their adjustment to and the treatment of the wider society are minimal and they are generally free to express their mannerisms, speech, and cultural ways, like religion. This is not to say that Indo-Guyanese do not face challenges in their new Indian communities. They still find it difficult to integrate themselves and lack the appropriate channels to negotiate for better treatment and available services and therefore feel constrained, confused, and demoralized in their new environment. It is not uncommon to hear remarks like, "I cannot believe our own Indian is treating us this way." The mere fact of leaving their own environment for a new one, irrespective of ethnic similarity, generally leads to stress and other psychological problems.

Interviews with scores of Trinidadians indicate that the treatment of Indo-Guyanese migrants varies according to their class. Upper-class

Indo-Guyanese migrants, such as doctors, lecturers, and other skilled personnel, are well received, though at times this class may feel excluded. Working-class Indo-Guyanese migrants—transient and illegal Guyanese—generally face the brunt of poor treatment in Trinidad. Their immigration status puts them in a precarious position within their new environment. They enter into these islands as unskilled migrants, which most CARICOM countries do not favor. They are treated as undesirable migrants who do not have the lawful legal status to stay in Trinidad, and they are generally poor and less educated. Ironically, these are the Guyanese who are most likely to move against enormous odds, including risking their lives, because of relative economic deprivation at home. The illegal status also prevents undocumented Guyanese from access to health care, decent housing, and official social services, as well as places them in vulnerable positions of abuse with employers. The *Trinidad Guardian* (2007) reported that Guyanese vendors are wreaking havoc in the Chaguanas market, threatening and assaulting local vendors. Mayor Surujrattan Rambachan said he called in immigration authorities several times to deal with the influx of illegal Guyanese migrants peddling their goods all over the market with no regard for regulations. These migrants will do practically anything to survive and succeed because of the lack of support in their new environment from the government and even from their own families. Many actually leave their families, who depend on them to send remittances to meet expenses like rent, bills, and food back home. One interviewee in Trinidad remarked that he has "three Guyanese working for him, one for yard, one for cleaning the house, and one for doing errands. But one gets smart and moved out and found a job in construction. Boy, them Guyanese after staying for a while in Trinidad, they find better jobs."[9] One common remark is that they place a burden on social services. Newspaper headlines across the English-speaking islands such as "T & T says Guyanese was not denied emergency medical Treatment" (*Jamaican Observer*, April 8, 2014) and "Mother decries treatment of Guyanese girl at Piarco" (*Stabroek News*, July 6, 2009) and reports that an Indo-Guyanese was denied health care and died reinforce the perception that Indo-Guyanese are not welcome in Trinidad. One must stress that a number of Guyanese have done well in Trinidad and have occupied important positions at the university, in the medical field, and in government.

INDO-GUYANESE IN BARBADOS

Of all places that Indo-Guyanese have migrated to, they face the worst treatment in Barbados. The Council on Hemisphere Affairs (COHA) reveals
that as soon as Guyanese migrants arrived in Barbados they were placed
on designated benches at the airport "in an effort to single out illegal Guyanese refugees."[10] Guyanese migrants in Barbados experience cultural and
racial discrimination, especially Guyanese individuals of Indian decent.
Discrimination is a common pattern in world migration when the inhabitants of sending and receiving environments are different culturally and
racially (see Marmaro 1990). Racial consciousness and social extremes are
rather acute in Barbados, going back to colonial times when light skin was
seen as a symbol of social superiority and dark skin quite the opposite.
The Indo-Guyanese, being overwhelmingly low-class and brown, fit in the
lower end of the inferiority category. Anti-Guyanese feelings have taken
many forms in Barbados. Politicians, inflammatory talk show hosts, and
newspaper editorials and reports, in an attempt to seek electoral capital and
gain political mileage, have often depicted newcomers as a threat to demographic, cultural, and national unity. Newcomers are perceived to infringe
on sovereignty and change racial composition. In an interview with Caribbean reporter Betram Niles, the former minister of state for immigration
in Barbados, Joseph Atherly, stated that a lot of utterances are being driven
into the minds of people that Barbados is being overrun by nonnationals,
particularly Guyanese and more specifically East Indian Guyanese. In the
same report, a Hindu Indo-Guyanese remarked, "there is discrimination
against Guyanese of all ethnic groups but this anti-Indian feeling seems to
be more pronounced and prominent" (Niles 2006).

Guyana's former foreign minister Carolyn Rodrigues-Birkett informed
the Guyanese parliament that those who were easily recognizable because
of ethnic features received the brunt of harsh treatment. The minister was
apparently making reference to Guyanese migrants of South Asian background. The honorary Guyanese consul to Barbados, Norman Faria, confirmed that Indo-Guyanese have been targeted in Barbados. The Guyanese
are targeted because the government at one time embraced a "Barbadians
First" policy ("Guyanese in Barbados Being 'Stereotyped'" 2009). The public
also believes that intolerable strain on their social services and the steady
influx of Indo-Guyanese would import the racial African–Indian tension
from Guyana to Barbados.

Unlike in Trinidad, where Indo-Guyanese migrants generally feel at home, the circumstance in Barbados is different. Indo-Guyanese migrants face more challenges of adjustment not only in Barbados but also in the predominantly Creole Caribbean. However, rural Indo-Guyanese tend to face most of the challenges of adjustment because of their insular upbringing as well as the lack of an established base in their new environment, with limited supporting networks. Like elsewhere in the Caribbean, particularly in regard to Haitians in the Dominican Republic, the Guyanese Indian population is of first-generation migrants who are not always cognizant and confident enough to push for rights and representation because of the fear of identification and deportation. There are some associations that deal with the difficulties of departing from home and that are concerned with the preservation of national culture through the revival and resuscitation of Guyanese events like holidays. These associations do not represent or address exclusive ethnic interests. They are symbolic and are not forceful enough to challenge bureaucracy and demand rights.

The mindset of Indo-Guyanese migrants in Barbados presents its own set of adjustment problems. They are economic migrants who are not interested in assimilating to Creole norms or sensibilities. Indo-Guyanese migrants are familiar with the Creole culture but are also skeptical and suspicious about it, especially those Indians who believed that they were hurt by Forbes Burnham's racial politics in Guyana. Moreover, Indo-Guyanese migrants are first-generation migrants who tend to retain their culture. Cultural retention among first-generation migrants is generally strong and persistent (see Clement, Singh, and Gaudet 2006, 291). The perception of these cultural ways is perceived by the host society to be antipatriotic. Mainly Creole, Barbados in turn identifies with Africanness and views the newcomers with suspicion because they are for the first time making contact with an ethnic group that is Asian Caribbean and different from their own. Moreover, members of the host society are in competition for jobs and are caught in daily struggles so are likely to misplace or misguide their feelings. Newcomers are feared to have come here to take over and consequently are exposed to ill treatment.

INDO-TRINIDADIAN AND INDO–ST. LUCIAN MIGRATION TO THE US VIRGIN ISLANDS

So far, the analysis of Indo-Caribbean intraregional migration has focused primarily on Indo-Guyanese migration to Suriname and Trinidad. The attention now is on Indo-Trinidadian and Indo–St. Lucian migration to the

US Virgin Islands. While the movement of Indo-Guyanese to Suriname and Trinidad was generally fluid, the movement of Indo-Trinidadians and Indo–St. Lucians to the US Virgin Islands is more regulated and restricted. Movements to the US Virgin Islands require a visa according to US immigration laws similar to those for Caribbean Indians who wish to travel to the US mainland. This explains why the population of Indians, not only from Trinidad and St. Lucia but from other islands as well, is relatively small. Since the requirements are more or less the same to travel to the US Virgin Islands and the US mainland, Indo-Trinidadians and Indo–St. Lucians prefer to travel to the latter rather than the former destination. Those Caribbean Indians who travel to the US Virgin Islands tend to do so under special circumstances, like looking for employment in the oil industry.

Furthermore, whereas the Indo-Guyanese movement to Suriname and Trinidad has been from within the semiperiphery, or the developing world, the movement of Indo-Trinidadians and Indo–St. Lucians has been from the semiperiphery to the core, or developed world. The US Virgin Islands are unincorporated territory of the United States. Conditions are not exactly like those in the US mainland, and in some ways are unlike those in Trinidad and St. Lucia, but residents of the US Virgin Islands receive privileges similar to those of citizens in the mainland—the protection of the US Constitution, social services, and high currency—which are absent in most English-speaking independent islands. Indo-Trinidadian and Indo–St. Lucian movement to the US Virgin Islands is essentially a South–North hierarchy of migration, which coincides with global movement. A majority of international migrants go to a country or destination with a higher level of human development than their own.

The reasons for the arrival of Indo-Trinidadians and Indo–St. Lucians in the US Virgin Islands are somewhat similar to that of Indo-Guyanese migration. These migrants were driven from their homeland because of economic hardships and social deprivation. A crisis in the oil industry in Trinidad in the 1980s led to an economic decline, while St. Lucia has not experienced sound economic development and is largely dependent on banana exports and tourism to generate revenue, both of which are at the mercy of international market trends. However, skilled Indo-Trinidadians have left on their own accord to take advantage of the lucrative industrial sector, such as opportunities at the former Hovensa Oil Refinery on St. Croix. A smaller number of Indo-Caribbean nationals from Trinidad and Guyana also migrated to the US Virgin Islands, bringing with them their culinary skills, which they subsequently used to set up appealing roti shops.

The arrival of these migrants coincided with an upsurge in growth and development in tourism, construction, and industry in the US Virgin Islands during the 1960s, which opened a wide array of opportunities for jobs and investment.

The size of the Indian population in the US Virgin Islands is estimated to be around three thousand. There is a notable cultural difference between Indo-Trinidadians and Indo–St. Lucians. The former have retained some major aspects of their Indian ancestral customs and culture while the latter have become totally creolized, even before migrating to the US Virgin Islands. The Indo–St. Lucians tend to fit easily into the US Virgin Islands' Creole society and have intermarried with the locals. Some Indians from Trinidad are either Christians or Muslims or nonreligious and generally associate and identify with the wider non-Indian Caribbean society. Those Indians from Trinidad that brought their Hindu religion with them have developed into an India–Caribbean religious hybrid group. These Indians from Trinidad and from India share the common Hindu religion, although there are internal differences. One interviewee from Trinidad hinted that "Indians from India think they are better than Indians from the Caribbean because they think they cultured," while one resident Indian on St. Croix said that he was "impressed how Indians from the Caribbean try so hard to maintain Indian customs," something he said he took for granted.[11] There is no established Indian community in US Virgin Islands, but India–Caribbean religious hybrid groups meet and mingle at the Cultural Center on St. Thomas and Shree Ram Naya Sabha Hindu Temple on St. Croix. They have also formed the India Association and broadcast a weekly Indian radio program. They live in well-to-do neighborhoods, such as in the secluded Judith Fancy and Hovensa complex on St. Croix. They send their children to prestigious private schools on the islands and to colleges and universities in the United States for post-secondary education.

Except for a majority of Indo–St. Lucians who occupied middle- and low-end occupations, Indo-Trinidadians, with their connection to Indians from India, have done well in the US Virgin Islands. This is because they entered the US Virgin Islands with technical skills. The Hindu Trinidadians have strong religious networks on and beyond the islands. Over time, they have acquired good financial standing and are no longer a displaced and disadvantaged minority group where they are exposed to constant incidents of racism and discrimination. They continue to embrace their cultural traditions and customs while simultaneously practicing selective assimilation. However, two events in recent times disrupted their tranquil life. The first was that the once-productive Hovsena oil refinery closed down in 2012 and the second was that some displaced ethnic groups, such as the "native Virgin Islanders," have voiced their position against recently arrived immigrants who they say have "taken over" vital resources. These groups express fears of marginalization and have been trying to influence changes to local constitutions to place restrictions on privileged immigrant groups such as Indians. An unknown number of Indians have left the US Virgin Islands since 2012.

A rare photograph of an indentured servant (Jane Bernhardt) on St. Croix, 1868–1873. Courtesy of Rana Bernhardt.

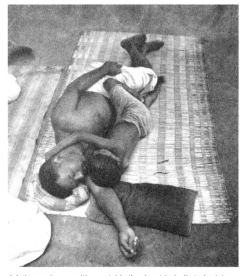

A father and son waiting outside the depot in India to be taken to an indentured colony. Courtesy of Mauritius Archives and Aapravasi Ghat Trust Fund.

An interesting emigration pass discovered at Indian archives in Mauritius showing that this boy was going to Skeldon, British Guiana. Courtesy of Mauritius Archives and Aapravasi Ghat Trust Fund.

A ship monument dedicated to the arrival of Indians in Georgetown, Guyana. Photo by the author.

An Indian woman vendor of Indo-Surinamese and Indo-Guyanese background at the New Nickerie market in Suriname, 2015. Photo by the author.

Indians from India celebrating Holi at Cramer Park, St. Croix, US Virgin Islands, 2015. Courtesy of Ravish Agarwal.

Indian Muslim women in Suriname. Courtesy of Maurits Hassankhan.

Kartik in Chaguaramas, Trinidad, 2016. Courtesy of Kumar Mahabir.

A Muslim gathering in Barbados. Courtesy of Sabir Nakhuda.

Indo-Surinamese duck curry festival in Holland, 2015. Courtesy of Chan Choenni.

The author presenting a paper at the Indentured Labor Route International Conference in Mauritius, November 2–5, 2014. Courtesy of Satyendra Peertum.

Chapter Five

INDIAN MIGRATION FROM THE CARIBBEAN TO EUROPE AND NORTH AMERICA

The previous chapter examined the movement of Indians within the Caribbean and showed that Indians did participate in this movement, which has gone undetected by analysts. Indians have contributed to their new destinations as well as to their former homelands. However, they continue to face bouts of discrimination and the challenges of effective integration into their new societies. This chapter analyzes the movements of Indians from the Caribbean to Europe and North America primarily following the Second World War, although references will be made to earlier periods. The first part of the chapter focuses on Caribbean Indian migration to Britain and Hindustani Surinamese, or Indo-Surinamese, migration to the Netherlands in Europe. References to Indian migration from the French Caribbean to France will be few, mainly of because of the paucity of literature in English and statistics on this movement. The second part of the chapter focuses on Indian migration from the Caribbean—Guyana and Trinidad—to New York and Toronto in North America.

SOME GENERAL PATTERNS OF INDIAN EXTRA-REGIONAL MIGRATION

For the most part, and at least up to the 1960s, Indian extra-regional migration has been an intracolonial movement, that is, movement from the colonies to the metropole. It is a movement from one less-developed region to a more-developed one and from a multiethnic Caribbean region to a mainly white society. The movement was one-directional—from the colony to the colonizer. For example, Indians from the British Caribbean migrated to Great Britain; Indians from the French Caribbean to France; and Indians from Dutch Guiana, now Suriname, to the Netherlands. This movement mirrors the economic mercantile system of the movement of goods from the colonies to the metropole. Like the mercantile system, any movement from the colonies to destinations other than the same metropole was deemed illegal and was discouraged through immigration laws. This pattern of migration continues, except that, since the 1960s with the introduction of strict immigration laws in Britain, new liberal immigration laws in the United States and Canada, and the formation of independent immigration laws in the former British Caribbean, the migration of Indians in the former British Caribbean has shifted from Great Britain to North America.

Initially, migrants from the Caribbean to Europe and North America comprised upper- and middle-class and skilled personnel, students included. But in the second half of twentieth century, the movement was driven by labor needs and attracted individuals from different stratas of society. (The movement to Europe has never been significant, although large numbers of Hindustani Surinamese live in the Netherlands. Large populations of Indians are found in New York and Toronto.) It was also the first time Caribbean Indians came in contact with a predominately white society. In the Caribbean, they were exposed to white individuals through the colonial government, civil service, disciplined forces, and the school system. But in Europe, in particular, they were exposed to all segments of white society as soon as they entered. While in the Caribbean the white personnel sought their cooperation and advice, in Europe the migrants were the ones asking for cooperation, acceptance, and help.

Before the 1960s in the former British Caribbean and before 1975 in former Dutch Guiana and currently in the French Caribbean, statistics on migration and ethnicity were not documented. Like the Puerto Rican movement to the United States, the British, French, and Dutch governments considered individuals in their respective colonies to be citizens and did not collect information on their movement or place them in a separate category in their census. This makes researching migration and ethnicity difficult.

CARIBBEAN INDIAN MIGRATION TO GREAT BRITAIN

It is not precisely known when Caribbean Indians began to arrive in Great Britain. Some former indentured servants who chose to stay in the Caribbean took the opportunity that emerged from the colonial system to receive educational training to fill colonial posts. For example, in 1916 the winner of the Guiana Scholarship was Balgobin Persaud, a son of an indentured Indian at Plantation Enmore. Persaud won the Primary School Scholarship and entered Queen's College then went on to Cambridge University with the Guiana Scholarship (British Guiana 1923, 18). This student movement was small and temporary. The migrants usually returned to the Caribbean after completing their education and training to work in the civil service. Nevertheless, this movement was important and status oriented. Those who had gone and studied in Great Britain were ambassadors and mouthpieces for future migration from the Caribbean. These migrants, upon returning, held a high status in their respective communities. Their education and training was valuable in helping Indians understand complex Western issues such as court proceedings and labor rights. This early extra-regional migration was male oriented and continued more or less into the 1960s and 1970s. When asked why she would not want her daughter to go overseas and study nursing, one Indian woman replied, "I do not want her to marry a blue-eyed man."[1]

Caribbean Indian migration increased gradually after the First World War. Emancipation from indentureship and settlement allowed Indians to make individual choices. As Indians began to see themselves as citizens, they entered into the school system and civil service within their respective Caribbean countries. This exposure and experience prepared them to take advantage of the free movement from the Caribbean to Great Britain and, to a lesser extent, within the British Empire. Unlike the first movement, these Indians stayed in Great Britain but they never formed a visible Indian community, although they attempted to reconstruct their homeland culture. The early Indo-Caribbean migration to Britain was a part of a larger Caribbean migration, mainly following Africans who were recruited directly by British Rail, London Transport, the post office, and the National Health Service in an attempt to rebuild war-torn Britain (Peach 1968, 20). However, specific circumstances in Guyana, such as the fear of an African Creole domination, caused Indians to migrate to Great Britain in the 1950s and early 1960s. These early immigrants were mainly urban oriented prior to leaving and had acquired some level of education that prepared them to deal with the challenges of a developed society.

Steven Vertovec thinks that about 2,750 Indo-Trinidadians and 5,414 Indo-Guyanese—an estimated eight thousand Indo-Caribbeans—are living in Great Britain (2000, 112). Other sources place the Indo-Caribbean population in Great Britain at around twenty-five thousand to thirty thousand. A majority of them live in the London area without a clear Indo-Caribbean residential area. These immigrants are scattered around London. One Indo-Caribbean Londoner informed me that "usually Indo-Caribbeans settle in places where there is a hub of activity, mainly around cities and towns. They are basically scattered throughout the North, South, and in the Midlands. Cities and towns that have a denser population of Indo-Caribbeans are Leeds, Bradford, Nottingham, Sheffield, Manchester, Birmingham, Southall, and Coventry" (Prashad 2015). By the 1980s, the Indo-Caribbean community in Great Britain became more noticeable, at least among the immigrant community from the Caribbean and former British colonies in Asia and Africa. They began to reconstruct Indian-Caribbean customs and practice Hinduism in the London area—similar to what their ancestors had done during the period of indentureship in the Caribbean. Some influential leaders came with the first migration wave of Indians to Britain, but over time influential leaders, mainly in religion, were born and bred in Great Britain. These individuals provided religious services—birth and death ceremonies, for example—for the dispersed Indo-Caribbean community in London. Indo-Caribbean community events were also promoted in the wider Caribbean community by the *Caribbean Times*, founded by Guyanese-born publisher Arif Ali, who is now the owner of Hansib Publications in London. In a telephone conversation, Ali recalled that when he arrived in London in the 1950s, there was no media outlet for Caribbean people in London, though they lived in the city in large numbers. He said this was unfortunate, and he began promoting Caribbean interests through local newspapers and eventually created a publishing house for Caribbean writers in England and the Caribbean (Ali 2015).

The urge to more or less replicate life in the Caribbean sprang from the experience of hostility from white British citizens and loneliness, so articulately revealed in Sam Selvon's novel *The Lonely Londoners* (1956). Like most nonwhite immigrants to Great Britain, Indo-Caribbeans also faced discrimination in employment, housing, and schooling. To deal with British hostility, Indo-Caribbeans formed associations with other ethnic groups, such as African Caribbeans, to achieve greater integration in Britain. Over time, and in search of their own identity, Indo-Caribbeans were able to reconstruct a Caribbean Hindu community and identity in the London area. This urge for one's own identity has produced unexpected outcomes. Indo-Caribbeans do not want to be labeled as black West Indians or South Asians. Because of this urge for a separate identity, one Indo-Caribbean female living in London says,

Indo-Caribbeans face great challenges with respect to integration and assimilation into British society. They are torn between Caribbean identity and South Asian identity and have difficulty adapting; therefore, they may feel marginalized. On the one hand [in some instances] there is an association of "Caribbean Identity" with black Caribbean only. On the other hand, South-Asians tend to ostracize Indo-Caribbeans because they are descendants of laborers and have been "creolized." In my opinion therein lies their greatest struggle; finding a balance between Caribbean Identity and South Asian Identity on an international stage. (Prashad 2015)

Indo-Caribbean children raised as British have identified marginally with their parents' Indo-Caribbean experience. It is not uncommon for children to root for British sporting teams while parents root for Caribbean teams. However, with the rise of terrorism so associated with the Muslim community and Britain's low tolerance for anything that resembles the Middle East or the Arab world, British-born Indians of Caribbean background find that they are not automatically accepted by the British, especially in the conservative North. They are often mistaken for being Muslims from Pakistan or the Middle East.

INDO-SURINAMESE OR HINDUSTANI MIGRATION TO THE NETHERLANDS

Indo-Surinamese or Hindustani migration to the Netherlands shows a similar pattern to that of the migration to Great Britain. The movement was dictated and determined by colonial ties and political and economic instability in the colonies. Similar educational structure, and to some extent, a similar culture, provided opportunities for upper-class Surinamese to pursue higher education in the Netherlands. This was really a movement, certainly before the Second World War, that attracted the Creoles who were more urbanized and more exposed to Dutch accruements than Hindustani Indians who were not interested in outward migration. The latter were more comfortable with their rural-based traditional ways and their non-Western values around family structure and religion. For example, they were comfortable with extended family patterns, Hinduism, and Islam. By the 1950s, however, they started to break out of their insular rural environment and migrate to Paramaribo, the capital, and then to the Netherlands. Like the Creoles, they saw migration as an opportunity for upward social mobility. Their migration, however, was small, but after the Second World War, especially the decade before 1975, Hindustani migration from Suriname to the Netherlands rose sharply, attracting urban and rural Hindustanis. Political instability and fear of a Creole takeover of the newly independent Suriname caused about thirty-six thousand Hindustanis to leave Suriname between 1971 and 1973 and settle in the Netherlands. Outward migration continued because of the 1980 coup, the civil war in the 1990s, and the withdrawal of financial support from the Netherlands, the United States, and other developed nations. Up to the year 2000, Suriname was almost a failed state. Everyone was leaving Suriname, and the preferred destination was the Netherlands. There are over 350,000 Surinamese of mainly Indian, African, and Javanese ethnic backgrounds living in the Netherlands. More than half of them are from the second-born generation. The current Hindustani population in the Netherlands is around two hundred thousand. The Hindustanis live mainly in Hague, Rotterdam, Zoeterneer, and Almere. The largest Hindustani community in the Netherlands (Little Suriname) is in The Hague and is estimated to be around fifty thousand people in size (see Bal 2012; Amersfoort 2011; Choenni 2011; *Focus Migration* 2007).

DUTCH INTEGRATION POLICY TOWARD HINDUSTANI SURINAMESE

The questions to be asked regarding Dutch integration policies are these: How did the Dutch government respond to this never before seen mass migration of people? What policies and programs were put in place? Were they fair? What is interesting is that the Netherlands has always experienced inward and outward migration. Before the Second World War, the predominant form of migration was outward, mainly to Canada, the United States, South Africa, and Australia. These countries were similar to the Netherlands in ethnicity and economic standing and, therefore, this pre–Second World War migration was lateral; there was little difference between sending and receiving destinations. After the Second World War, inward migration became the predominant migration trend. The Netherlands attracted immigrants from former Dutch colonies as guest workers to rebuild the war-torn country. Indo-Surinamese or Hindustanis migrating to the Netherlands made up a sizable portion of these *allochtonen* (people from elsewhere, mainly non-Western people). Until the 1970s, the Netherlands did not have an integration policy because it was thought the guest workers would return home. There was no urgent need to integrate these immigrants into Dutch society other than offering them the amenities associated with welfare recipients: basic housing, medical care, food stamps, and so forth. The immigrants were comfortable with this situation since they were convinced that they would return. However, a majority of guest workers remained in the Netherlands. Like so many European governments of the day, the Dutch government also was consumed by a Malthusian fear of overpopulation. This fear was supported by the notion that nonwhite immigrants were more difficult to integrate and were often engaged in drugs and crime (see *Focus Migration* 2007).

In the case of Surinamese immigrants, two events changed this lack of integration policy. The first is that the sudden push for Surinamese independence by the Creole leader Henck Arron caught the Surinamese by surprise. In 1974, Arron stated that Suriname would be independent in 1975. The Dutch government was very eager to grant independence, believing this would restrict immigration from Suriname to the Netherlands. Surinamese were, however, Dutch citizens, and a constitutional change was required to create a separate nationality for them. That did not happen. The Dutch government was forced to make a concession allowing Surinamese to travel freely to the Netherlands from 1975 to 1980. After this date, Surinamese migrants would have to apply for a visa to travel to the Netherlands, which placed greater restrictions on their movement. To beat the expiration date, thousands of Surinamese migrated to the Netherlands. The second event that changed the lack of integration policy was that the Surinamese turned out to be disadvantaged immigrants, living in segregated enclaves and experiencing high levels of unemployment, crime, and depression. The Dutch government responded by offering socialized housing at a low cost. One unique situation was that the Dutch government was building a number of high-rise apartments for Dutch working-class citizens but experienced difficulties in attracting these individuals, who preferred to live elsewhere. The vacant high-rise apartments were subsequently occupied by Surinamese immigrants at a low cost. Over time, some Surinamese have moved out to other enclaves, but a distinct Surinamese community has formed around these high-rise apartments, such as the ones in Bijlmermeer. The Dutch government also introduced a policy that focused on integration while allowing immigrants to maintain their own immigrant identity or former homeland customs and culture.

By the 1990s, the Dutch government's integration policy shifted from cultural retention to full integration to Dutch values in education and in the workplace in particular. One source claims that "the change in integration policy was part of a larger change in discourse on state policy from the rights of citizens to the duties of citizens. In the 1980s and 1990s the welfare state was facing a crisis: the number of people on welfare had become too large relative to the working population" (*Focus Migration* 2007, 5). What this meant was that for effective integration to happen the immigrants must play an important role, such as acquiring knowledge of the Dutch language to prepare them to not only understand Dutch society but to take advantage of opportunities in it. The Dutch government made it mandatory for all immigrants, except those from the United States and a few European countries, to take six hundred hours of language and Dutch societal orientation classes. The 9/11 attacks in the United States, however, changed Dutch integration policy from liberal to conservative. The current focus is less on pillarization or multiculturalism and more on emphasizing and institutionalizing Dutch values because of the belief that the immigrant culture, Muslim in particular, is not really a source of enrichment but an impediment to integration.

INDO-SURINAMESE COMMUNITY FROM WITHIN: PROGRESS AND PROBLEMS

So far, we have examined how the Dutch government responded to the inflow of Hindustani Surinamese. In comparison to other Western European countries, the Dutch policy of integration was admirable, especially before 9/11. After this tragedy, Western countries, including the Netherlands, have applied tougher integration policies on immigrants, namely a confirmation of Western values rather than an embrace of multiculturalism. But how did the Hindustani Surinamese respond to the Dutch policy of integration? To answer this question, it is instructive to examine their community and family structure in the Netherlands. The majority of Hindustani Surinamese migrants in the Netherlands following the first decade of Surinamese independence were from the rural areas outside of Paramaribo and New Nickerie, with a peasant lifestyle, strong extended families, and a Hindu and Muslim religious orientation. These individuals were exposed to Dutch culture since they attended schools that were conducted in Dutch, but they lived a hybrid lifestyle intermixed with urban Dutch values and their peasant way of life, with more emphasis on the latter. This experience was common among the colonized Caribbean people around the 1960s.

The first wave of Hindustani Surinamese migrants to the Netherlands was largely composed of the more urban-oriented upper class. These first immigrants from Suriname to the Netherlands did fairly well because they arrived in the Netherlands with a greater level of education and capital than later immigrants. They never established a community to which new immigrants from Suriname were attracted for assistance and accommodation. This happened later, with the arrival of Hindustani Surinamese from various backgrounds. The Hindustani immigrants of early postindependence Suriname to the Netherlands were really pioneers who had to reconstruct or export their community and lay the foundation for themselves and for later immigrants. As stated above, the Dutch government assisted with its integration policy. Later migrants naturally went to the established communities to be among relatives for support. The internal social structure of migrants also helped with the development of many Hindustani communities in the Netherlands. A majority of these immigrants who arrived in the Netherlands were over thirty years old or were married and had children. They also had strong kinship connections before arriving in the Netherlands. Once their communities were established with the assistance of the local government, they began to transplant their homeland community by building their own cultural infrastructure to meet their own needs. Poet and singer Raj Mohan (2008, 50) explains this experience eloquently in his poem "Poets of Memory" when he says that even though he left Suriname for a long time, the mud from his feet from the fields of Suriname can still be seen when he walks on the pavement of Holland.

Within decades there emerged a string of Hindustani temples, ethnic networks, and associations in the Netherlands with their own internal structure amid some assimilation into the wider society. These early immigrants focused on maintaining their Hindustani Surinamese way of life and on achieving materialistic values such as jobs, regular incomes, home ownership, cars, and self-employment in business. Professor Ruben Gowricharn (2009) says that Hindustani Surinamese immigrants are a "model minority" in the Netherlands when compared to other nonwhite immigrants (Turks, Moroccans, and Antilleans). Their achievements are far greater in education, income, and ownership of business. Their involvement in crime and drugs is lower. Their general well-being is much better, as they experience fewer health issues, such as hypertension, strokes, and heart attacks. They are also more fluent in the Dutch language because of a longer history of exposure to it in their homeland before arriving in the Netherlands. However, except for lower-class Dutch citizens, Hindustani Surinamese immigrants in the

Netherlands trail far behind white Dutch citizens in occupational, educational, wealth, and health status, mainly because they have been fairly new in the Netherlands and they face bouts of discrimination and marginalization from the predominantly white society. They are virtually invisible in the political sphere in the Netherlands (see Gowricharn 2015). In spite of this, Professor Chan Choenni believes that Hindustani elders in the Netherlands are happy. He writes, "that the overwhelming majority of Hinduostani [sic] elders is happy in Holland is not only related to this attitude (Santokham Paramsukhum)—if you are satisfied with yourself, everything will be all right—but also to the Dutch welfarestatism. The excellent Dutch medical service and social security system, and the state pension for every elder in The Netherlands guarantees their material wellbeing" (2013, 55). Like so many recently arrived immigrants from non-Western or colonial societies to mainly white, developed countries, Hindustani Surinamese immigrants in the Netherlands have brought problems with them, or they have created or confronted new ones. The mere fact of leaving home without knowing fully about the new destination brings loss, pain, and nostalgia. One study finds that suicide, alcoholism, abuse, and depression were high among first-generation Hindustani Surinamese in the Netherlands—higher than all other ethnic groups, including white Dutch citizens (Brijmohan 2016, 149–78). The challenges of dealing with two societies, the breakdown of close relations, and the different values between the first and second generations were some factors that caused social ills. The first generation tends to live in cocooned communities, while the second is more acculturated to Dutch values. With increasingly higher levels of education, these younger Hindustani have not only moved out mentally—more emphasis on the Internet and social media, less on the traditional first-generation cultural values—but physically to other non-Hindustani communities through jobs and marriages with second-generation Hindustani and other ethnic groups, preferably white Dutch because it signifies upward social mobility. However, the second generation is still connected to the first-generation communities through family gatherings for leisure and other events, such as funeral services.

CARIBBEAN INDIAN MIGRATION TO NORTH AMERICA

Whereas the Indian movement to the Netherlands was exclusively from Suriname, the movement of Indians to North America—the United States and Canada—was from a number of former British Caribbean colonies as well as from Suriname. The Indians from Guyana and Trinidad, however, have dominated this migration, although there has been a small and steady movement of Indians from St. Lucia and Jamaica. This latter movement has not developed into a recognizable community in North America like those of Indians from Guyana and Trinidad. There is, for instance, a community named Little Guyana in Queens, New York, which is predominantly Indian. The Africans from Guyana and Trinidad tend to settle in and around Brooklyn. While Indians from the islands with small Indian populations such as Grenada, St. Vincent, and Belize, for example, sometimes end up in Little Guyana, they generally move to non-Indian communities in North America. The reason for this is that these Indians share little commonality with Indians from Guyana and Trinidad. They have more commonalities with the Creoles, which they generally bring to North America. They tend to seek out communities that are more African Caribbean oriented or non-Caribbean communities, rather than those that are Indian influenced.

Notwithstanding the early movements mainly of students and professionals, the Caribbean Indian movement to North America started in the 1960s, precisely when Great Britain closed its immigration doors to West Indians. The new immigration law specified that West Indians already living in Great Britain could sponsor spouses as well as children under sixteen years old, but all others were banned from entering Great Britain. Meanwhile Canada and the United States opened their immigration doors to West Indian immigrants in 1962 and 1965, respectively. In 1962, Canada removed the nonwhite immigration policy based on social, ethnic, and racial backgrounds and began accepting immigrants based on educational and occupational qualifications (*World Migration Report* 2000, 238). Put differently, Canada decided to accept nonwhite immigrants based on skills rather than racial characteristics. In 1965, the United States removed the differential national quotas and embraced a policy or a system in which provisions applied equally to prospective immigrants regardless of where they were born ("US Immigration Policy" 1981, 87). The consequence of these reformed immigration laws was that the movement of West Indians shifted from Great Britain to Canada and the United States. Notably, however, the reformed immigration laws did not interrupt the continuous movement of Indians from Suriname to the Netherlands or from the French West Indies to France. Colonial and contemporary ties make it easier for those immigrants to adjust and settle in the "mother land" than in North America, where the language is different.

The Caribbean Indian movement was driven by economic and political instability, especially in Guyana. By 1989, an estimated 80 percent of Guyanese were living in poverty. The Caribbean Indian movement is also connected to other factors. The formation of an Indo-Caribbean diaspora in North America became a natural attraction to Caribbean Indians as many became aware that a support base existed upon arrival. Positive news of a better life filtered from North America back to the Caribbean and also encouraged outward migration. From the 1980s onward, a majority of lower-class Indians in Guyana, and to some extent in Trinidad, saw their future not in the Caribbean but in North America. Fears of marginalization and discrimination found an outlet in migration. The normal modes of migration such as sponsorship and being issued visas increased alongside illegal departure from the Caribbean to North America and marriages, including fake ones, between the sending and receiving destinations. In Guyana, for instance, migration has been an investment and a way of life. People saved their money to buy airline tickets or to pay anyone who would take them illegally to North America. There was actually an illegal migration route from Guyana through the Caribbean to Central America and then to the United States. Interviews with some former Guyanese illegal aliens in New York have confirmed this illegal migration. There was also another illegal movement from Canada to the United States, commonly known as "boring the border." One former illegal Indian in the United States recalled his entry into the US from Canada through Buffalo.

Twelve of us, including one small child in 1982, were taken into a van driven by one man from Guyana. Following us was a semitruck driven by a Trinidadian. He was smoking pot before he left Canada and his reasoning for doing so was that he wanted to look tired to the immigration officers at the border crossing at Buffalo. About five miles before we got to the US–Canada border we all jumped out of the van and went into the back of the semitruck. The same Trinidadian driver told us not to say a word and he would honk the horn when we were about to reach the border. The tarp on the trailer of the truck was lowered halfway to give the impression that a few things were at the front of the trailer and if the immigration officers wanted to check they would have to jump onto the trailer and walk forward. Well, when the truck stopped at the border crossing we could hear the immigration officers talking to the driver, but then the little girl who was about six years could not bear it anymore and started to cry. Luckily the mother put her hands over her mouth. God was with us that day. We crossed into New York and after about five miles we got back into the van and was driven to New York City.[2]

At least a fourth of Indians who went to North America in the 1980s did so illegally using the routes mentioned. The steady outward migration of Caribbean Indians has had a direct impact on their departed communities. Their majority status in places like Guyana has been reduced and, correspondingly, so has their power base in government, since ethnic groups in some Caribbean countries tend to vote on the basis of ethnicity as opposed to policies. Those who are leaving seem jaded; they have become demoralized with failed government promises and performance. By contrast, outward migration has led to a better living standard for migrants in North America, amid sacrifice and frustration. In some ways, these migrants have been uprooted twice: first in India and second in the Caribbean, and they are aptly dubbed "twice migrants." We are not sure about the size of these twice-migrant communities in North America, but the rough estimate is that there are seven hundred thousand Caribbean Indians in North America, five hundred thousand in the United States, and two hundred thousand in Canada. The figure is higher—somewhere over one million—if second-generation and mixed-heritage Indians are considered. Caribbean Indians might be counted in the 2020 population census in the United States as a separate category of people.

CARIBBEAN INDIAN CULTURAL RETENTION IN NORTH AMERICA

It is impossible to cover all aspects of the Caribbean Indian experience in North America since migrants arrived in large numbers starting mainly from the 1960s. Some patterns are obvious, however. Caribbean Indians have yet to make significant inroads into the political system in which they live. They do have some say in the political affairs of their community but not like that of white North Americans or immigrant groups who have had a longer period of residence. But over time, Caribbean Indians in North America will become meaningful political participants in their community affairs. Similarly, observations from continuous visits to Queens, New York, and Jersey City, New Jersey, for over two decades indicate that their economic success is questionable. What a majority of the first-generation Caribbean Indians have done is to really focus on attaining material goals. In some ways, they can be described as economic or materialist immigrants. Three reasons account for this description. First, many entered North America empty-handed or indebted to families and friends who assisted them financially when they arrived. These immigrants' primary focus was finding a job to pay off their debt and finding a secure economic base, such as decent housing for themselves, to avoid embarrassment and derision from the overseas Guyanese community. Second, a majority of them, from Guyana in particular, arrived with little education and limited skills. Their goal was to find a job that would allow them to survive and save, which meant they took the first low-paying job available. Some have retained these low-paying jobs for over twenty years. An interviewee remarked that one Guyanese Indian man "has been parking cars ever since he arrived in New York twenty-five years ago. He will be punished later in life because that job does not have good benefits."[3] Another interviewee claims that "self-motivation among Indo-Guyanese in Jersey City is very low and they are satisfied with little achievements but brag about it."[4] Third, a majority of Caribbean Indians own cars and houses but through loans and mortgages. While many have paid off their houses and cars, they have not invested in education for themselves in order to achieve greater goals in society. Educational achievement is happening with the second-generation Caribbean Indians, as many have attended top universities in North America and have high-level jobs. One Caribbean Indian in New York says,

> Even though you make it, the problem is not physical but psychological. We in Guyana come from a majority culture and we are a minority subculture in New York. You have to give up a lot, and still the main society is not aware of this. But the good thing is that you can be part of the American dream and live a simple and industrious life like our indentured ancestors.[5]

Although the number of Indians doing well will rise, it remains very small in comparison to those who have remained lower class in North America. However, in pursuing their economic goals, the lower classes have always maintained the principle that they are working and making sacrifices for their children. Almost everyone who was interviewed stated that they were making sacrifices for their children in North America as well as those left behind in the Caribbean so that those children would have a better life than they. One male Indian security guard at a hospital in Queens, New York, said, "When I first came here I used to go to bars to have a good time but when

I woke in the morning after I would find my pocket empty. I would spend most of [my] paychecks at the bars. Now I stopped that and I am paying for my daughter to go college." He continued: "America is a great place. It gives you what you want. If you want a car, you can get [it]. If you want your street repaired you can have it done. But it has a way to take things back from you. They will charge for it or get it back through taxes. This is one smart country."[6] It should be noted that an unknown number of Caribbean Indians have achieved great economic success in North America, but many more are not economically successful. The latter are not necessarily poor, but they are in the process of building strong families and strong connections to the wider North American society.

Caribbean Indians have, as they have done in Guyana and Trinidad, retained remarkable aspects of their culture in North America. There are, of course, thousands of Caribbean Indians who have become North Americanized, especially the second generation, and have not retained Caribbean Indian culture or customs that revolve around Hinduism. There is absolutely no doubt that there is a distinctive Caribbean Indian culture in North America. The question is, How have Caribbean Indians been able to retain their culture and customs in North America amid some changes in their social structure? What is even more interesting is that they have retained a culture that resembles India's in North America, even though many have not gone to India and have not made any meaningful connections with the Indian community from India in North America. Moreover, no government-initiated integration policies, such as the ones the Hindustani experienced in the Netherlands, exist in North America. Ethnic groups are not forced to conform to any particular cultural norm or process and they are left alone to develop or dismiss cultural ways as long as they do not violate any laws. Even if there were a cultural integration policy in North America, it would have to face the reality that in a globalized world identities and cultural reconstructions of immigrants and diasporic populations are always shifting and redefining themselves. The continuous contact and cultural exchange through air travel and the Internet between the sending and receiving enclaves have allowed Caribbean Indians to retain their culture in North America. New immigrants, for example, bring old ways and knowledge that are diluted in the Indian diaspora. Likewise, technology and social media make it easier to foster and restore cultural ties. The immigrants' experience in the new environment has also driven them to retain their culture. Bouts of discrimination and exclusion and the experience of being labeled as something other than their own Indian ethnicity in the host society have pushed them into restoring and retaining their own culture (see Premdas 2004). Almost all interviewees share two common characteristics in North America: discrimination and exclusion. What is most noticeable among them is that the longer they stay in North America the more aware of their position and treatment in the host society they become. Initially, these immigrants were silent in their new subworld. They are now more active in asserting their new space.

So what have Caribbean Indians retained in North America? Apart from working, saving, and sacrificing daily for years, in some cases, a lifetime, Caribbean Indians have shown an enormous desire to preserve their culture that revolves around the elastic form of Caribbean Hinduism. What this means is that the Caribbean Indian form of Hinduism is more socially flexible than Hinduism in India or even that of Indian immigrants from India to the United States. The caste social structure is certainly missing, although the ideology of it has been retained symbolically. The lower classes may not receive the same treatment or sit in the same section of the temples as upper-class Indians. Caribbean Indians have built a number of temples in North America or have joined already established mosques, which can be described as their nerve center. The mantra appears to be that wherever and whenever there is a sizable population of Caribbean Indians, there are temples. While this is expected in New York and Toronto, which have large populations of Indians, some may be surprised to see Caribbean Indian temples in Minnesota, Georgia, Florida, and Schenectady in New York, among other places. These temples provide the basis for the reconstruction and retention of Caribbean Indian culture in North America. This is where associations are formed and extended outward to the wider community. This is where various festivals are planned and practiced and then taken to the wider community. Thousands generally attend the yearly festivals of Phagwah, or Holi, and Diwali as well as chowtal singings in Queens, New York, as they do in the Caribbean. The celebration of festivals has provided a deep anchorage for restoration and continuation of Caribbean Indian culture in North America. The Caribbean Indian culture is not only restricted to religion but is also expressed in the streets, such as on Liberty Avenue in Queens where Indian businesses excel: sari stores, roti shops, bakeries, restaurants, Caribbean fish and vegetable markets, as well as yearly regional and village reunions (Mahabir 2015).

Like so many new immigrants to an environment different from their own, Caribbean Indians in North America also face internal social problems. Some of these problems, such as poor upbringing, weak family and community bonds, and personal family disputes, have been transferred from the Caribbean to North America. Some other problems, such as alcoholism and spousal abuse among the first generation and drug use, dropping out of school, and unplanned pregnancy among the second generation, are common in Caribbean Indian communities in North America, although they aren't as prevalent as in some ethnic groups. Certainly more networks beyond their own community are needed to tackle these social ills. They need to be more cognizant about the benefits associated with political participation and community enhancement and development.

INTERNAL MIGRATION OF CARIBBEAN INDIANS WITHIN THE NORTH AMERICAN DIASPORA

One main drawback of writing about Indian Caribbean migration to Europe and North America is that there are practically no studies on the movement from one diasporic community to another. For instance, there is no study on the movement of Hindustani Surinamese in the Netherlands to the United States or the movement of Indo-Caribbeans in Britain to the United States or the movement of Caribbean Indians in North America to Europe. It would seem logical to assume, given that these Caribbean Indian communities in Europe and North America have been in existence for about fifty years, there has to have been some movement. Moreover, migration between these developed countries is less cumbersome than migration from the Caribbean to Europe and North America. Migration between developed countries is fluid since it is assumed that these migrants present fewer problems. The movement is seen to be more of a benefit than a burden to sending and receiving destinations. Furthermore, these Indian diasporic communities are connected by families, which would naturally generate some movement among them. There are, of course, some barriers such as language differences that discourage intradiasporic migration. Arguably, there are movements within the Indian diaspora in Europe and North America, but the size of these movements is unknown. Likewise, there have been internal movements of Caribbean Indians within Europe and North America. For instance, there has been migration from The Hague to other small towns and cities in the Netherlands, from London and Toronto to other towns, and from New York to other states. Like the movements within the diaspora, we do not know the size of this movement. However, there has been one noticeable movement of Guyanese Indians from Queens, New York, to Schenectady, New York, that deserves a brief discussion.

The 2010 census estimates that there are about twenty-three hundred Guyanese residents in Schenectady, a town that is located about 160 miles north of New York City. Field research, however, indicates that the Guyanese population there is around seven thousand and growing. By 2020, the Guyanese population there will most likely be around ten thousand. About 90 percent of the Guyanese population in Schenectady is of Indian ethnicity. Schenectady was not a town to which people migrated and settled; people outwardly migrated. The town was hit hard by the closure of its main employer, General Electric, and by pollution. Boarded homes and closed businesses were a common sight. Most Guyanese immigrants who came to the United States stayed in New York City. This changed, however, after 2000.

Mayor Al Jurczynski became aware of how the Guyanese population has transformed Queens, New York, and wondered if they could do the same with Schenectady. The mayor went to Queens and brought busloads of Guyanese individuals to Schenectady on a weekly basis in 2002 and asked them to buy the boarded-up and abandoned houses at a low cost, ranging from $5,000 to $1. Within a short period, these houses were transformed into beautiful buildings. Business has returned. Guyanese residents have opened various grocery stores and restaurants. They have built a few Hindu temples and formed a cricket team. This internal Indo-Caribbean migration in the United States was driven by a number of factors. First, many wanted to move away from the fast-paced life of a big city and live in a better environment for their children, although Schenectady has a high crime rate and a reputation for police brutality. Second, housing is much more affordable in Schenectady than in New York City. Third, many were influenced by word of mouth that Schenectady is a better place to live than New York City. This growing Indo-Guyanese community is in the process of building itself in Schenectady. The community has done well in restoring some sections of Schenectady for itself (see Kershaw 2002). The community is relatively peaceful and is not known for crime. There have been, however, some murders among Indo-Guyanese families. Like in Queens, New York, Indo-Guyanese will continue to transfer their culture to this region of the state. In the process, they have been exposed to toxic waste, which the town is yet to take care of fully, as well as hostility from other groups who thought the former mayor was favoring the Guyanese and ignoring them. The transference of Guyanese culinary culture has caused unexpected outcomes. One study shows a high prevalence of diabetes in the Indo-Guyanese community in Schenectady, caused mainly by unhealthy eating habits and an immobile lifestyle (see Hosler et al. 2013).

RETURN AND TRANSNATIONAL MIGRATION

While there have been a number of studies on the return migration of Caribbean nationals from North America and Europe, there is practically none
on the return migration of Indo-Caribbean people. Also, no study exists
on the transnational migration of Indo-Caribbean people. Transnational
migration is defined here as individuals involved in a regular migration
between two or more places. They do not live permanently in one place but
may live six months of the year in one place and six months of the year in
another place. We do know, however, that Indo-Caribbeans have engaged in
return and transnational migration on a regular basis. We do not know the
numbers that are involved in these migrations. A rough estimate would be
no more than 5 percent, that is, probably less than fifty thousand of the one
million Indo-Caribbeans living in Europe and North America. To clarify,
return migration does not mean short visits and vacations but rather the
movement back to the former homeland to live at least for three to five
years or permanently.

Why would Indo-Caribbean people want to return to the Caribbean?
Some Indo-Caribbean people return home because they have achieved
some level of economic, educational, and material success that would give
them a satisfactory lifestyle in their native homeland. They have acquired
enough finances to buy a parcel of land on which to build a house or
start a business or not work at all. Others return because they are disap-
pointed with their overseas experience. They have had a hard time trying
to integrate with the host society and see no real reason to remain. Still,
some return home because of visa controls that do not allow them to stay
beyond the authorized period of time. These are mainly students and
business people. Some individuals return simply because of the aging
process, as they would like to retire in their homeland, particularly if
they have property, investment, or family there. Older siblings are sometimes obligated to return home to take care of aging parents. The love of
home, strong nationalistic feelings, as well as the avoidance of long and
harsh winters may also stimulate return migration. Even conflicts within
families abroad may lead to return migration. Indo-Caribbean people also
remigrate because of conditions in their homeland. If the political, social,
economic, and medical conditions improve, then there is likelihood of
them returning home. Finally, the global recession, which started in 2008,
forced many Indo-Caribbean people to return home. Of all the Indo-
Caribbean people abroad, Indo-Guyanese are less likely to return due to

political, economic, and social instability coupled with a poor health care system in Guyana (Roopnarine 2013).

Return and transnational migration have had a profound impact on Indo-Caribbean communities in Guyana, Trinidad, and Suriname. The positive aspect is that returning Indo-Caribbean people introduce new skills, ideas, and techniques, as well as capital, which are much needed for growth and development. Returning Indo-Caribbean people generally have a positive demonstration effect, which the local population tries to emulate: for example, in their office demeanor and computer skills. These returnees are important sources of investment as their remittances have led to unprecedented levels of infrastructural development. These returnees are inadvertent innovators or facilitators of change. The negative aspect of return and transnational migration is that the home governments do not meet the expectations of returnees. They are not well paid and are placed in jobs that do not make use of their overseas training. They are also not placed in important leadership positions to make significant changes. The returnees are also maladjusted to the traditional ways of thinking because of the long time spent away from their homeland. This is particularly true of deportees.

Generally speaking, the impact of extra-regional migration on Guyana, Trinidad, and Suriname is manifold. These countries have experienced a brain drain, that is, the loss of skilled and educated personnel such as doctors, lawyers, nurses, teachers, and technicians. Outward migration from these countries has reduced human capital, which in turn stymied growth and development. The social cost has also been incalculable. Indo-Caribbean migrants generally leave their families behind, including children, who often lose their main source of support. The responsibility is then shifted onto relatives who generally have limited resources themselves to cope. The years of separation translate into children who grow up ignorant of the contours of their parents' faces. On the positive side, the extra-regional movement to developed countries certainly led to an Indo-Caribbean diaspora, the scattering of discrete and distinct subcultural communities. These microcommunities have contributed significantly to Guyana, Trinidad, and Suriname by way of remittances, which are not recorded by ethnicity. Overall statistics for Guyana reveal that remittances have increased substantially from $27 million in 2000 to $266 million in 2009 (see Orozco 2002). In 2010, Guyanese migrants remitted $374 million, and this figure is expected to increase over the next few years as the economy recovers from its precrisis levels. Inbound and outbound money transactions were valued at an estimated

$196 million. Remittances account for 20 percent of Guyana's gross domestic product and continues to play an important role as a source of foreign exchange, reducing poverty as well as providing for household costs such as electricity, education, and health bills. Similar patterns have been noticed in Trinidad and Suriname.

Chapter Six

NONINDENTURED INDIAN MIGRATION TO THE CARIBBEAN SINCE WORLD WAR II

The previous chapter examined the migration of Indians from the Caribbean to developed countries in Europe and North America. This was the first major movement of Indians from the developing to the developed world and constituted a noticeable Indian diaspora, which has contributed significantly in not only shaping but also preparing Indians in both destinations for the ongoing challenges of globalization. Indians were not left behind. This chapter analyzes the movement of non-resident Indians from India to the Caribbean after the Second World War, although references will be made to the initial movement of Indians since the First World War. Although Indians have migrated to almost all of the Caribbean islands, the focus will be on their movement to Guyana, Trinidad, and Suriname, mainly to compare and contrast their movement and settlement with that of former indentured Indians. The focus will also be on the movement of Indians to the US Virgin Islands and Barbados. These islands did not receive a significant number of indentured Indians before the arrival of non-resident Indians (NRIs), which presents the opportunity to analyze how these recent migrants with no plantation experience fare in these islands.

GENERAL VIEWS OF THE MIGRATION OF NON-RESIDENT INDIANS TO THE CARIBBEAN

In his book *Deep South*, travel writer Paul Theroux was impressed by the size and diversity of the Indian population in the southern United States and by its starling diversity of occupations and living conditions. He writes:

In a landscape of whites and blacks, the most conspicuous person I saw was this man, my first in the South, the owner-manager of a motel, a dot Indian with a caste mark on his forehead rather than a feather Indian. Motels, gas stations, convenience stories: [*sic*] they had a lock on them, and the first one stood for so many I was to find. One of the whispers in the South is that whites sold these businesses to Indians as an act of defiance, in order to keep them out of the hands of blacks. I met hundreds more Indians, nearly all of them from the state of Gujarat in western India, many of them recent immigrants. (2015, 25)

In a few days, the writer saw unexpected aspects of Indian life in an un-expected environment, the Deep South. His observations are pertinent to the analysis of NRIs in the Caribbean. First, most NRIs who are in the Caribbean do not come from or form the lower class in their own country or in the Caribbean. They are from the professional and business class. They have successfully extended this status in the Caribbean. Second, most of them came to the Caribbean from all over India but especially from some specific areas, such as in Gujarat, western India. Third, the comment that Indians have been successful in attaining prosperity relatively quickly after arrival because of racism against blacks is not a whisper in the Caribbean. It was echoed widely during the indenture period and in some cases around Emancipation Day in modern-day Guyana. The argument is that the white plantocracy brought in indentured Indians to undermine the bargaining power of free blacks for better wages and housing arrangements. This does not seem to be the reason NRIs have achieved some level of prosperity, although there are some tensions between Indians and blacks in Barbados and on St. Thomas, US Virgin Islands.

NON-RESIDENT INDIANS IN TRINIDAD, GUYANA, AND SURINAME

There is no precise date as to when NRIs arrived in Trinidad, Guyana, and Suriname. The basic understanding is that some arrived during the indenture period in the nineteenth century as religious travelers spreading Hinduism and Islam. Their purpose was to provide religious inspiration and support for the indentured community on the premise that these laborers were uprooted from their homeland and taken to a foreign land where their religion was unknown. Toward that end, religious travelers ensured that the laborers were protected from religious abuse and conversion and that they continued their religious practices in the Caribbean. While over time the indentured community produced its own religious leaders, however few, these early religious travelers played a role in aiding indentured Indians to retain at least some aspects of their religion in their new domicile. The flow of these religious travelers was sporadic and small, not more than two to three hundred throughout the whole indenture period. Their impact or intended impact was more significant than their numbers. Their tradition has remained as a part of the Indian experience in the Caribbean. Indian religious travelers and now religious gurus and leaders continue to come to the Caribbean, while Caribbean-born Indians continue to travel to India for religious education and training.

By the end of indenture in 1920 there was a small group of NRIs in the Caribbean. How they got to the Caribbean is not clear. It is believed that some were sailors; some answered advertisements in local newspapers that took them to Brazil to cut timber; some came to do business. The latter was the most popular reason for them being in the Caribbean, as evidenced by their continued participation in business—mainly selling Indian clothes, religious items, and groceries. Some of these early immigrants did not come directly from India but were already in Latin America and the Caribbean region. Through conversations with their customers and among themselves they became more knowledgeable of the history of their new surroundings, especially with regard to extending their business beyond their immediate base. Some migrated from predominantly non-Indian Latin America and the Caribbean to Guyana, Trinidad, and Suriname because of the large Indian populations in these countries. In his book *From Bengal to Barbados*, Sabir Nakhuda provides an interesting account of the first NRI immigrants to Barbados. He writes: "There were many Bengalis in Trinidad who were itinerant traders, selling textiles, dry goods, jewelry and other items door to door on a credit basis. It is possible that during his short stay in Trinidad, Bashart Ali learnt itinerant trade and decided to migrate to Barbados for a greater financial reward" (2013, 20). This pattern of migration for business opportunities continues today. A young Indian male managing a SAFCO store in New Nickerie, Suriname, declared the following in a July 25, 2015, interview:

I have been in New Nickerie for eight years, and SAFCO is the only Indian store in this town. The only Indian business. I am from Mumbai (Bombay) and I did not come from India to this place. I was in Trinidad and then I realize that business can be good here because of the Indian population. The people are kind and there is no problem, but the people food here is different and they have a different concept of Indian food. I do not like Surinamese Indian food. We prepare our own food.[1]

Unknown descendants of the first wave of NRIs to Guyana, Trinidad, and Suriname have blended with descendants of indentured servants through intermarriage and residential assimilation. Elsewhere in the Caribbean, they have intermarried with the Creole population or even migrated to Europe and North America.

The major flow of NRIs to the Caribbean began after India achieved independence in 1947. Independence provided India the opportunity to establish ties with countries that had large populations of Indians to enhance growth and development as well as to develop stronger cultural connections. Nowhere is this initiative as noticeable as on various Indian High Commission websites in countries with large Indian populations, such as Guyana, Trinidad, and Suriname.[2] High Commissioner of India to Guyana H. E. V. Mahalingam, on the occasion of the 67th Republic Day in February 2016, said in a speech, "to consolidate cultural links, the Indian Cultural Centre has been functioning in Guyana since 1972 and during the four decades, a large number of Guyanese have benefitted from its yoga, dance and music classes" ("India Pledges Support" 2016). Over in India, the *Times of India*, a news magazine, ran this: "helping upgrade a much-needed mortuary, sending a Ramlila troupe to exchange ideas with the local troupes there or providing expertise in renewable energy—India is actively engaging with its large diaspora in the small and distant countries of Suriname and Guyana in meaningful ways" ("Connecting with Suriname, Guyana" 2015). Not all NRIs in the Caribbean are associated with the Indian High Commissioner's office on diplomatic duties. Actually, there are four categories of NRIs: diplomats, professionals (doctors and teachers), businesspeople, and religious leaders. The population of these NRIs is small, ranging from three hundred to one thousand each for Guyana, Trinidad, and Suriname. In spite of their category and size, they share four fundamental characteristics. The first is that they live a life of privilege and prestige. Their residences are located in well-to-do neighborhoods and their children attend the best schools in the host country. Their main aim is to send their children to the United States. The second is that they see themselves as immigrants first rather than as residents and have little meaningful contact with the wider society other than their occupational connections and Indian-related activities.

The third is that they consider themselves better than Indians in the Caribbean because they believe Caribbean Indians have lost true Indian values. For example, Brahmins in the Caribbean are not seen as a pure group, as skillfully expressed by Brinsley Samaroo in many conversations with the author: "they are Brahmins by boat not by birth." The fourth is that they do not generally marry someone or let their children marry someone from the Caribbean.

NRIs are more visible and progressive in Trinidad than in Suriname and Guyana. Trinidad is more developed and therefore Indians are associated there beyond diplomatic functions. Doctors and professors earn higher salaries in Trinidad than in Guyana and Suriname. Moreover, during the repressive People's National Congress (PNC) regime in the 1970s and 1980s in Guyana, ties were almost severed with India, although they have been restored since 1992. Trinidad is the NRIs' favorite place to be in the former Indian indentured Caribbean. This was revealed at the Indian Diaspora Conference in Trinidad in 2015 and reiterated at a reception at the Indian High Commissioner's residence. Field notes and my attendance at both events revealed the following, some already stated. There are about one thousand to fifteen hundred NRIs living in Trinidad, which translates into about two hundred families. Some are diplomats, doctors, academics, traders, and business personnel. There is also a small student population. They are located mostly in Port of Spain and in Chaguanas, the business district. Unless they speak or dress for an occasion, it is difficult to distinguish them from Trinidadian Indians. NRIs have good professional relations with Trinidad, but they are not deeply connected culturally, which, paradoxically, is one of the mission statements of the Indian High Commissioner's Office.

There is a paradoxical relationship between NRIs and descendants of Caribbean Indians. NRIs do not recognize the achievement of these early pioneer Indians of maintaining some semblance of Indian identity, and they engage in debates as to who is a real Indian and who is not a real Indian. The position of the NRIs is that if one is not born in India, one is not a real Indian. By contrast, some NRIs are often stunned to see that Indians in the Caribbean have maintained their Indian culture. Some NRIs deeply admire Trinidadian Indians for holding on to their past Indian culture, something NRIs have taken for granted. The NRI population is predominately male-oriented, or appears to be so, since most of the females, including wives, stay home, according to one Indian interviewee. NRIs generally visit India once a year, but the visit is always for leisure or to get away from island life. Some go back to meet their spouses through arranged marriages, although some male interviewees said they do not mind marrying a Trinidadian Indian. Those that have children prefer them to study and grow up in India or the United States, while some are notably homesick.³

INDIANS IN THE US VIRGIN ISLANDS

Indian migration to the US Virgin Islands was connected to uneven capitalist development during two and half centuries of colonialism in the then Danish West Indies. Labor shortages after the abolition of slavery led to the arrival of the first wave of Indian migrants to the US Virgin Islands in the second half of the nineteenth century, in 1863. The British crown allowed Denmark to import 321 indentured Indians from India ("Distribution of Indians on Danish St. Croix" 1863).

The second wave of Indian migrants to the US Virgin Islands occurred a century later, following World War II. The migrants who came from the East were Sindhis (Sindhi is a denomination of Hinduism) who originated in Pakistan but relocated to India when the country was granted independence in 1947 from Great Britain. These Indians settled mainly on St. Thomas. Some migrants came from other regions of India, such as India proper, but settled in the United States and Puerto Rico for a while and eventually migrated to the US Virgin Islands. Political turmoil and economic hardships during early post–Indian independence caused Indian migration to the US Virgin Islands. Other Indian migrants made a conscious choice to migrate by evaluating and analyzing prospects of doing well in business. The size of the Indian population in the US Virgin Islands is estimated to be around one thousand, some six hundred on St. Thomas and St. John and four hundred on St. Croix out of a total US Virgin Islands population of 106,405. The size of the major ethnic groups in the US Virgin Islands is as follows: blacks or Africans, 70,369 (66.1 percent); Hispanics or Latinos, 18,504 (17.4 percent); whites, 14,352 (13.5 percent).⁴

Indians send their children to prestigious private schools on the islands and to colleges and universities in the United States for postsecondary education. It is difficult to state specifically the economic status of these Indians in the US Virgin Islands in terms of wages. However, it is possible to surmise that skilled Indians in the private sector earn on average at least twice as much as the US Virgin Islands' per capita income of roughly $17,000. Certainly, the fact that Indians dominate the microeconomic sector, especially on St. Thomas, and are in a position to give back about $300,000 to various institutions in the US Virgin Islands suggests that they have to be in some sort of good financial standing (see below).

Indians in the US Virgin Islands tend to embrace a national homeland identity rather than a Virgin Islands identity. Simply put, a national identity is the expression of a sense of belonging to a nation-state and sharing common traits such as language, culture, and religion. A national identity is the highest attachment of group loyalty, superseding and surpassing other rival identities. Such a feeling can be expressed in a multitude of ways, ranging from carrying the flag of a nation to going to war. Indian national homeland identity in the US Virgin Islands is expressed through the acknowledgment, reconstruction, reenactment, and celebration of significant political events and social practices of India. The India Independence Day celebration, for example, is well planned, organized, and executed on St. Thomas annually at the upscale Marriot Frenchman Reef Beach Resort. The media and guests are invited from all classes of society and the consul general of India to New York, the governor of the US Virgin Islands, senators, and members of the business community attend. The first event at this celebration is the Vande Mataram dance, a bow to the motherland, followed by other dances, drama, songs, folklore, and speeches. At the 2008 Independence Day celebration on St. Thomas, Deputy Consul General of India to New York Ajay Gondane said, "without roots in the cultural past, a tree cannot grow strong in new ground" (Bostwick 2008). This sentiment is expressed through a weekly East Indian radio program on St. Thomas. On a regular basis, Hindus worship at the Shree Ram Naya Sabha Hindu Temple in the affluent La Grande Princess area on St. Croix. National Indian festivals like Holi and Diwali are celebrated, bringing Indians closer together. Unlike in India and in Trinidad, Guyana, and Suriname, Indian festivals in the US Virgin Islands are celebrated mainly indoors and in some cases at public parks. It is uncertain why this has been the case, but the consequence is that only a small section of US Virgin Islands society is aware of Hindu celebrations on St. Croix in particular. As far as is known, the media has not covered any Hindu celebrations on St. Croix. However, from 2007 to 2010, when Diwali was held at the Hindu Mandir, or temple, former Governor John P. de Jongh as well as a number of non-Hindus attended.[5]

Of greater significance is that these activities demonstrate a desire to resuscitate, reassure, and reinforce solidarity among Indians and to foster a greater understanding of Indian culture in the wider US Virgin Islands society. Nowhere is this urge to maintain a homeland identity more evident than in an adage relayed by Consul General of India to New York Prabhu

Dayal in his keynote address to some four hundred attendees at the India Independence Day celebrations on St. Thomas in 2010: "You can take the Indian out of India but you cannot take out India from the Indian" (Pancham 2010). This event is generally attended by Indians from India and local politicians but not by Indians from Trinidad, reflecting some sort of insularity between these two groups when the Hindu religion is not involved.

For now, Indians are not forced to maintain a homeland national identity in the US Virgin Islands. There are many reasons for this. First, there is a lack of governmental input toward social and territorial ethnic integration. Ethnic groups are basically left alone to determine and dictate their own identities. Apart from government-sponsored and supported cultural activities such as carnival, and a few private cultural and historical organizations, any creative political actions required to transform the fragmented and disunited population into a coherent nationality are practically absent in the US Virgin Islands. Even if the US Virgin Islands had an organized cultural integration plan, it would have to contend with the gradual decrease of nation-state control and direction over every aspect of society in an ever-globalizing space where identities of migrants and diasporic populations are always shifting and redefining themselves. Second, the length of residency among the Indian immigrant group in the US Virgin Islands also leads to a national identity. Those who have been in the US Virgin Islands only for one or two generations show a stronger feeling and attachment to their homeland. They do not identify with the predominantly plantation-derived Creole identity, especially those Indians from India. Their identity has not significantly been transformed into that of a Virgin Islander. Instead, they display an attachment to or identification with their ancestral or recently departed homeland, a determination to protect their language and religious beliefs and to limit the overall impact of Virgin Islands' culture and mannerisms on their children and communities. Finally, in the age of advanced technology, Indians can easily contact their homeland on a regular basis through the Internet and media. Actually, many Indian nationals in the US Virgin Islands subscribe to television programs from India. This fluid and technological connection allows them, with some degree of selective assimilation, to maintain rather than give up their national identity in a foreign land. However, no ethnic group, or more so immigrant group, can exist in isolation. There has to be some relationship with the host society, and to that we turn.

THE RELATIONSHIP BETWEEN INDIANS AND US VIRGIN ISLANDS SOCIETY: PARTICIPATION AND PERCEPTION

Ever since Indians began living in the US Virgin Islands some four or five decades ago, they have been participating and contributing to their new environment in a variety of ways. Initially, their participation benefited themselves, as they built a cultural center and a Hindu temple and established department stores. Then their participation widened to the broader US Virgin Islands society, especially to individuals and institutions in need. They have also responded resoundingly to various international disasters directly affecting the US Virgin Islands. In 2005, when the tsunami struck the Indian continent, the India Association on St. Thomas immediately launched a local fund and food drive to assist the victims. The association raised about $50,000 (Bedminster 2005, 3). Similarly, when the Haitian earthquake occurred in 2010, the India Association donated $23,000 to the US Virgin Islands Haitian Relief Fund. The then acting president of the association, Pash Daswani, informed the media that he had sent an e-mail to its seventy-member business community requesting contributions to ill-stricken Haiti, and the members responded in the affirmative. A check was eventually presented to Governor John de Jongh on local television (Cooper and McCoy 2010, 4).

The most impressive contribution, however, has been to various institutions in the US Virgin Islands. Since the 1980s, this small association has given over $300,000 to the US Virgin Islands. The sum of $50,000 went to the University of the Virgin Islands (UVI), while $100,000 was pledged to Charlotte High School, $100,000 to Charlotte Kimelman Cancer Institution, and $20,000 to Lockhart Elementary School (Fields 2008, 2). The association declared that its humanitarian work is not based on handouts but aims to empower the less fortunate and bring relief to the vulnerable. It states further that it is interested in contributing to the society in which its members live. The US Virgin Islands government welcomes the association's contributions, especially at a time when the territorial government has been struggling to cope with socioeconomic development and a scarcity of resources.

The association has also been a critic of local government for imposing higher taxes and not providing much-needed infrastructural resources to conduct as well as protect businesses. In July 2011, the India Association and the business community discussed their concerns with the senators. Chief among them were increases to gross receipts taxes, the lack of enforcement of existing laws relating to business, excessive water and electricity bills, and unfair competition and tax payment (Lewin 2011, 4). The owner of Lucky Jewelers and a member of the India Association suggested to the senators that, to boost revenues, the territory must lure overnight guests because they are the ones who spend the money. He said small things such as fixing potholes, repairing sidewalks, adding public restrooms, and providing better transportation make a good impression and attract guests (4). Moti Sujanai, another member of the India Association and manager of Diamonds International, spoke about how he was attacked and threatened by barkers (individuals who attempt to exhort people in public to buy from particular stores) who lured customers away from his business. He said he called the Virgin Islands police department repeatedly, but the situation remained the same (4). The fact that the meeting was jointly hosted by the Virgin Islands Legislature and the St. Thomas–St. John Chamber of Commerce and held at the India Association Cultural Center and that the association members' remarks were so blunt testifies to the amount of power and influence this small group has acquired in a relatively short period. This power came from two sources: East Indians, like their white American and Arab counterparts, generally come to the US Virgin Islands with wealth and invest wisely. Secondly, they virtually control the St. Thomas duty-free port, with its robust tourist influx and trade, which has proven to be very lucrative for business.

There is no doubt that Indians work very hard to achieve a high economic status and they are in a position to give back to the US Virgin Islands. Their continuous contributions have caused Lt. Governor Gregory R. Francis to declare that the India Association gives from the heart (Bostwick 2008). The US Virgin Islands, however, is a rather complex place, especially to recently arrived business immigrants who do not share an African Creole identity. Victimization of newcomers, especially those coming in with wealth, as well as the outsider/insider mentality, is rife in the US Virgin Islands. How much of this will be directed toward Indians can only be revealed over time.

NON-RESIDENT INDIANS IN BARBADOS

Unlike Guyana, Trinidad, Suriname, and the US Virgin Islands, where there have been established populations of Indians, Barbados did not receive a significant amount of Indians before the arrival of NRIs. The few invisible Indians that were on the island came mainly from Trinidad. Immigration to Barbados was checked by overpopulation and high unemployment, and until recently, migration in Barbados has been predominantly outward. The arrival of Indians in Barbados presented an interesting challenge as to how the native Creole population would deal with the new arrivals, so different from themselves. The second wave of Indians to Barbados and the wider Caribbean has no plantation experience. It would be interesting to find out how these Indians have been received by the majority Creole population with limited Eastern cultural exposure. Likewise, how have NRIs responded to their society? Are the ethnic tensions between blacks and Indians in Barbados similar to those in Guyana, Trinidad, and Suriname?

NRIs began to arrive in Barbados in the early twentieth century in small numbers. Although they came from all over India, they were mainly from West Bengal, Gujarat, Sindh, and South India. There are also Indians from mainly Guyana and Trinidad. The Gujarati are Muslims, while the Sindhis are Hindus. This ethnic group is called Sindhis because they can trace their origin to Sind, which is now Pakistan. When Pakistan was declared an independent Islamic state, the Hindu Sindhis fled to India and elsewhere. There are an estimated two thousand East Indians in Barbados, with around twelve hundred Gujarati, 350 Sindhis, and the rest South Asians and Indo-Caribbeans (see Hanoomansingh 1996; Nakhuda 2013). Except for South Asians who migrated to Barbados in the latter quarter of the twentieth century as professionals, nearly all of the early NRI immigrants came with itinerant trading skills and some money to do business. Some did not come directly from India but from other regions in the Caribbean and Latin America after receiving news that Barbados was a friendly and peaceful place to live and do business. Author Sabir Nakhuda states that the first East Indian to live in Barbados was a man named Bashart Ali Dewan. Dewan left India around 1910 for Trinidad and then migrated to Barbados. From his Bridgetown base, he sold goods to Creole Bajans all over the island from door to door, often on a credit basis. He apparently could not afford to send for his wife in India, so he married a number of Bajan women in Barbados according to his Islamic beliefs. He eventually fathered many children and then suddenly disappeared from the island in 1937, supposedly fleeing from the 1930 labor riots and from debt burdens (Nakhuda 2013, 21–23).

The story of Bashart Ali Dewan is very informative in helping us to understand the early development of the Indian society in Barbados. A majority of the early immigrants were single males who chose to marry Creole Bajan women and, in the process, created a new Indian-Creole ethnic group. There is no particular name given to these offspring, like *dougla* in Guyana and Trinidad. The Indians who are born in Barbados are called Indo-Bajan or Bajan Indian. The early immigrants lived a flexible way of life, incorporating

Creole cultural and culinary elements. However, while they did not impose their Islamic and Hindu beliefs on their Creole spouses and mixed children, the early immigrants retained some fundamental aspects of Islam, such as not eating pork and abstaining from drinking alcohol. Through hard work, frugal spending, sacrifice, and the ideology of working for themselves, East Indians rose from humble beginnings to become a formidable merchant class in Barbados. By the twentieth century, not only did their population grow to be around three thousand due to migration from India, high birth rates, and similar ethnic marriages, but they have also come to dominate the business sector in Barbados. This economic stability and social security allowed East Indians to form associations among themselves, join other Bajan associations, participate in politics and non-Indian events, develop kin-based residential clusters with their own places of worship (mosques and temples), send their children to high-level schools, and practice endogamous and exclusive norms. They have been doing all this without losing their religious identity. They integrate themselves selectively into Bajan society.

What is so interesting, however, is that although the Gujurati and Sindhis came from the same region and from the same ethnic background, their experience in Barbados is not necessarily the same. Certainly they share similar characteristics as newcomers and business-oriented people, but how these characteristics have played out in Barbados demonstrates that these ethnic groups are more exclusive rather than inclusive of each other. In some ways, this is expected since both groups belong to the two most extreme religions in India, in which separation rather than integration is the norm. The tensions among these groups are not as intense as in India, at least openly. The Sindhis have had a longer business tradition and have come to own many businesses in Barbados, especially on Swan Street. They are more cohesive through the reproduction of Hindu norms and beliefs. They are more likely to associate with other ethnic groups in Barbados, either through offering employment opportunities or religious associations with South Asians and Indo-Caribbeans.

INDIAN AND CREOLE RELATIONSHIPS

Indians have made a significant contribution to Barbados. Their success in business allowed them to provide credit as well as to offer job opportunities to lower-class Creoles. Indians are also serving in many professional capacities, such as in the medical, law, and political fields. One of their contributions made national headlines soon after Barbados achieved independence in 1966: "A specially craft chair was presented as a gift by the Indian High Commissioner, Mr. Muni Lal, to the Speaker of the House of Assembly, Mr. J.E.T Brancher, on the 24th April 1968" (Nakhuda 2013, 148). The idea behind the gift was to foster stronger ties with Barbados and the emerging East Indian community on the island.

The relationship between Indians and Creoles has not always been amicable and respectful but has sometimes been precarious. To illustrate, I will analyze what is sung in two songs by Bajan Creoles, "Curry Soca" and "2009." In "Curry Soca," the message is that Indians are dedicated people who work hard and save their money, unlike Creole Bajans, who tend to be careless with money and life in general. In the song "2009," the message is to inform the Bajan government that Indians are taking businesses from Creole Bajans, and by the year 2009 they would control the business sector of Barbados if some immigration restrictions were not placed on Indians. Subsequently, some Indians were targeted but without serious ramifications.

The artists of both songs are crediting Indian mores and chastising Creole ways as being loose and careless but warn that Indians are in Barbados to take over the retail sector. In an ethnographic study on ethnic minorities' relationships with Creole Bajans, Haaja Degia revealed some similar perceptions on Indian-Creole relations in Barbados. The author's findings are: (1) Creoles are consumer oriented and materialistic; (2) their family patterns are unstable; (3) they have an inability to save and defer immediate needs and delay gratification, while Indians are thrifty and hardworking. Creoles blame themselves for not achieving more because of a lack of cohesion and solidarity (Degia 2007).

The biggest challenge Indians currently face is how their Islamic and Hindu religions will be accommodated in a mainly Christian and Westernized Barbados. They have made tremendous economic and social strides in accommodating themselves, communicating, and expressing their religious faith as well as fostering in-group cohesion, especially to the newer generation. In doing so, they have become valuable residents. However, their differences (Muslim and Hindu calendar, prayer, dress, gender perceptions) with Bajan Creoles as a minority, in particular, have commanded respect and resentment. How they will balance this binary opposite will depend largely on their continuous tri-focal ways, which are (1) embracing their homeland customs; (2) adjusting to Bajan society; and (3) total assimilation.

Chapter Seven

INDIAN IDENTITY IN THE CARIBBEAN

The previous chapters examined the various phases of Indo-Caribbean migration. This chapter focuses on how migration has led to the formation of different types of identity among resident Caribbean Indians as well as those living abroad. Two alternative analyses of Indian identity in the Caribbean are presented. The first alternative is Coolieology, that is, a theoretical as well as a practical framework that argues that Indians in the Caribbean have not overcome the indignities of indenture. The second alternative is a multipartite approach that argues that Creole identity (Euro-African) does not apply to a majority of Caribbean Indians. The identity of Indians in the Caribbean can be conceptualized on an ethno-local, an ethno-national, a trans-Caribbean, and a global level. Within all four there is a sense of struggle to maintain these identities. Some overlaps also exist in this multipartite structure of Indian identity. To understand these two alternative analyses of Indian identity, it is instructive to observe how Indian identity has evolved as well as examine some prevailing thoughts and trends related to Indian identity in the Caribbean.

INDIAN IDENTITY DURING INDENTURE

Indentured Indians brought with them to the Caribbean a form of identity that revolved around their religion—Hinduism and Islam—and their social structure: mainly caste, a strict form of social stratification into which individuals are born to specific stations of life and remain until death. These forms of identity were powerful in terms of guiding day-to-day activities and life in general among indentured Indians in their homeland (see Bayly 1999; Basham 1964). However, upon the Indians' arrival in the Caribbean, these forms of identity were immediately challenged. The Caribbean plantation system identified with and revolved around Western values, which were the opposite of the Eastern values of the migrants. Western plantation values were motivated and guided by production and profit as well as the practice of Christianity, while Eastern values were motivated and guided by caste rules such as purity and rank and the practice of Hinduism and Islam. The differences between the two value systems whenever they clashed had an enormous impact on the Eastern value system for two fundamental reasons. The Western plantation system was more powerful, and the Eastern value system was a transplant without any firm grounding in the new environment. The outcome was that the migrants had to adapt to or resist the plantation system to find a place for themselves. In the islands where Indians were the minority, they were quickly absorbed into the wider society with relative ease, largely due to the exposure to Western education, the work of Christian missionaries, as well as the desire of the migrants themselves. These Indians in St. Lucia, Grenada, and St. Vincent, for example, have lost practically every aspect of their homeland identity described above. They are considered to be Creole, although there have been efforts in these islands to revive some aspects of their ancestral customs.

The situation was different in countries where Indians had formed the majority population, for example, in Guyana, Trinidad, and Suriname. They maintained aspects of their homeland culture but also assimilated to Western norms. This sort of hybrid identity was possible, especially during the second half of the indenture, because of isolation from the wider Caribbean society, land ownership, and their large numbers. These characteristics provided the base and support for cultural persistence, selective assimilation, and cultural resistance (see Klass 1961). Nevertheless, the Indian social structure of the caste system was totally transformed into a class system. Hinduism and, to a lesser extent, Islam had become somewhat elastic religions among the migrants and lost some consecrated and conservative aspects. For example, it was possible for a low-caste person to become a pundit or a religious leader, something that was impossible in India. That Indian homeland identity had changed during indenture is hardly surprising. The Caribbean plantation was a culturally fertile place where conditions and thought patterns were challenged, reconstructed, and reevaluated—as evidenced during slavery. Immigrant laboring groups had to conform or contribute to the regimen of plantation life, which produced patterns of cultural change although some cultural continuity remained. The question is not whether Indian identity experienced change during indenture but how much of it changed and to what degree and in what direction. Were Indians successful in retaining or transferring some of their homeland identity? Or have Indians become creolized like most of the Caribbean?

INDIAN IDENTITY DURING THE POSTINDENTURE PERIOD, 1920–1980

The arguments surrounding what sort of identity Indians assumed in the Caribbean after indenture ended have revolved around two opposite positions. Some have argued that, through resilience and reconstruction, Indians—for example those in Guyana, Trinidad, and Suriname—have been able to maintain some remarkable aspects of their homeland identity, with some modifications, in their new environments. The argument is that in spite of pressure to change, Indians were determined to maintain their identity in the Caribbean (see Niehoff and Niehoff 1960; Klass 1961). Much of the cultural retention and persistence of Indians was born out of the conditions on the plantations. The planter class placed Indians in isolated communities to prevent unity among the laboring class, who the planters believed would cooperate to challenge plantation conditions. To deal with underdevelopment and the plantation policy of isolation, Indians formed reciprocal relations among themselves, or what anthropologist Morton Klass calls fixation ties; that is, Indians bonded irrespective of religion and status to cope with plantation conditions. They drew inspiration from their homeland culture—religion, feasts, festivals, and folklore—to adjust to new surroundings, which remarkably did not lead to truncation but to the transplantation of Indian ways in the Caribbean. Arguably, then, the displacement from India and isolation in the Caribbean provided opportunities, not obstacles, in the struggle for cultural retention and persistence (Davids 1964; Smith 1962; Despres 1968 Malik 1971).

By contrast, some have argued that Indian culture has experienced enormous change since Indians arrived in the Caribbean. They have not been able to maintain or integrate their Indian customs in the Caribbean. The caste system, hook swinging, and fire walking, for example, did not survive the crossing from India to the Caribbean. Some customs that have survived, such as the extended family living under one roof, continue to experience change. The multigenerational household survives today not because of social customs as in India but rather because of economic necessity, and even then it may last for only one generation. Like other colonized people, Indians in the Caribbean were displaced by the exigency of indenture that destabilized their family institutions. Their dire need to respond and react to local conditions in the Caribbean in order to survive caused much change in their social structure (Nevadomsky 1980a and 1980b; Clarke 1967). By the end of the Second World War, the Caribbean had changed so much that many countries had embarked on the path of decolonization, which opened up opportunities for the colonized in labor movements, politics, education, and leadership roles in the private and public spheres. Central to these changes was the call for individuals to embrace nationalism rather than ethnicity and "former homeland culture" as a way forward. Indian languages, for example, had no place in the national agenda. To be able to take advantage of or be prepared for nationalistic opportunities, Indians had to embrace the Caribbean's standard languages of English, Dutch, and French, even though in Suriname Indians have maintained their Hindustani language. There was no deliberate drive to suppress Indian customs. They had, and still have, more value in the private domain, but these private customs have also experienced change. It is not uncommon to find one person in an Indian home who does not speak Hindi or who is a Christian and the rest are Hindus or who is the only one that attended high school and was exposed to Western forms of education.[1]

It would be myopic to conclude that Indian culture and identity is a monolithic entity with firm boundaries. Apart from the rigors of plantation life, Indians entered the Caribbean with the hope of economic gain, even if that meant severing ties from their homeland as well as ties within the Indian community in the Caribbean and adapting, adjusting, and acquiring the advantages of Westernization. Arguably, however, Indian ways simply did not disappear into the wider Caribbean social system. Certainly, an estimated third of the Caribbean Indian population is Hindu while the remainder is of Muslim, Christian, or other faiths. Nevertheless, Indians have been able to maintain manifest and latent functions of their identity in the Caribbean, although not exactly as they would in India. Added to this analysis, some have argued that Indians display selective expressions of their culture and identity. That is, in the workplace and in public places they express feelings of being a part of the society in which they live through participation, but by the end of the day they retreat to their own separate enclaves and live by their own ways that are not exactly like those of the wider society. For example, many practice Hinduism. Some scholars have labeled this mode of behavior as the plural model (Smith 1965). Groups mix and mingle in the open but display their own core values in private. One criticism of this model is the failure to acknowledge the shared values of Indians with other Caribbean ethnic groups emerging from the common plantation experience.

CREOLIZATION AND COOLITUDE

By the 1980s, the discussion of Indian identity in the Caribbean shifted from the binary opposite argument of cultural persistence and assimilation to creolization. The core of the creolization argument is that since Indians have lost their caste system and have now adjusted to the Caribbean class system, their experience is similar to African creolization. In the Caribbean context, creolization is a process whereby postemancipation Caribbean people have developed a way of life different and distinct from that of their original homelands—Europe, Africa, and Asia. Accordingly, new forms of social organization, language, religion, and values emerged and old ones were reshaped. European and African traditions were merged into a system that was neither totally like Europe or Africa but uniquely Caribbean, with more emphasis on African ways or Africanness (see Smith 1965). For example, an average African person in the Caribbean may look like someone in Africa or Europe but does not speak like someone in Africa or in Europe unless he or she has lived in one of those regions for some time. Creolization emerged mainly from European and African traditions in the Caribbean. For many Africans creolization is not only a form of identity but is a concept or a place to begin to recover the Africa that was lost during slavery. Though Indians also have experienced aspects of European and African traditions, that is, creolization, through, for instance, the educational system, its application to Indians as a form of identity is limited in Guyana, Trinidad, and Suriname—home to the majority of Indians in the Caribbean. The first limitation is this: To say Indians have embraced a creolized identity would imply not only that they have experienced a social process that is Euro-African but that they have given up their Indianness or any customs associated with India. Many Hindus with an Indian identity live in the Caribbean. The second limitation is that the concept of Creole identity ignores the spirit of agency among Indians and suggests that they are incapable of retaining their Indian customs in the Caribbean. One critic wrote that "creolization is pro-black, marginally white and faintly Indian" (Roopnarine 2009b, 98). Coolitude emerged out of this mislabeling of creolization. The concept of

Coolitude was first suggested by Franco-Mauritian poet Khal Torabully in the early 1990s. Coolitude is a new concept to honor the forgotten experience of Indians, or "Coolies," from the departure from India to the sea voyage and in the new Caribbean environment—not in relation to lost India or the idealized mother India but to encounters and integration with other cultures in the indentured Indian diaspora (see Carter and Torabully 2002). Torabully explains Coolitude:

> In a nutshell, coolitude is a vision of a modified, enriched humanity springing from the indentured experience. In a broader sense, it mirrors the reality of migrations, namely based on labor, which is an ageless phenomenon. In this process, the indentured enacts one of the most challenging human experiences when he/she meets with other languages, cultures, imaginaries and when he/she adapts, devises strategies to preserve original cultures, to create new homelands and to develop multiple identities. This construction means that out of the indentured past is devised a dynamic vision of the world that allows one to think of diversities with a view of promoting more understanding in human societies. From this dynamic experience, a *humanism of diversity* is evolved, a philosophy through which the original land/voyage is engaged in a complex process of retrieval and negotiations with diversities. (Roopnarine 2016, 291)

Authors such as Viranjini Munasinghe (2001) and Aisha Khan (1993) have also argued that Indian culture and identity has evolved in the Caribbean in such a way that Indians have come to see themselves in a variety of ways. Some Indians have come to identify themselves with North American culture even though they have never visited that place.

DOUGLARIZATION

Dougla was a term developed in India to describe the offspring of African and Indian persons on the subcontinent. It was brought from India to the Caribbean. A dougla is a mixed person of African and Indian heritage in the Caribbean, mostly in Guyana, Trinidad, and Suriname. The word, meaning "mix," is of Hindu origin. Douglarization, which describes the mixing of Africans and Indians, began when Indians arrived in the Caribbean as indentured servants. Today, an estimated 20 percent and 12 percent of Trinidad and Guyana's populations, respectively, are dougla. While douglarization has grown and has certainly become a form of identity in these countries, the concept is still ambiguous, and its level of acceptance varies according to time and place. Historically, and especially during indenture, the mere presence of douglas was regarded with a sense of shame that was born out of the tensions between the Africans and Indians and was perpetrated mainly by the ruling European class to ensure their security. A dougla person represented bastardization, an embarrassment to ethnic loyalty and cultural patrimony. However, a dougla person was accepted more in the African than in the Indian community for two reasons. Africans have been in the Caribbean longer than Indians and have experienced racial mixing, free or forced, as part of their Caribbean experience. By contrast, Indians arrived in the Caribbean with a caste structure that encouraged insular ethno-relations such as endogamy. The practice of these customs did not all survive in the Caribbean, but the ideology of ethnic exclusiveness did. To maintain the traditional cultural norms (such as arranged marriage) of their departed homeland, Indians went to great lengths to protect themselves from racial mixing. Those Indians who did mix normally had close relationships with Africans or had been at the lowest end of the Caribbean class structure and distant from the everyday life of Indians. Bridget Brereton argues that the practice of rejection of other cultural norms among Indians emerged from the desire to protect the Indian culture from being absorbed into the Creole culture (Brereton 1993, 51).

Whenever douglarization occurred there was this question of acceptance, which is not normally associated with other forms of racial mixing, like, for example, between Indians and Europeans in Guyana or Trinidad. The level of acceptance does not begin with the dougla offspring but with the mixed couple. If the woman is an Indian, she is most likely to be ostracized by her Indian family, sometimes for life. One dougla girl remarked that when her Indian mother eloped with her African father, her Indian family told her not to come back, and she did not go back to her family for over thirty years, although her offspring did visit.[2] One Indian woman from Trinidad who was living with an African man in the US Virgin Islands in 2008 said that if she went back to Chaguanas, Trinidad, with her African partner the community would "laugh and mock" her. She would be considered a low-class person for partnering with an African man. Likewise, in a heated argument in one Indian family in Guyana, a man said to one of the women who was dating an African man, "no other man na dey for you to tek," implying that any man other than an African man was suitable.[3] By contrast, if the man is an Indian, he will most likely be able to enter both communities—African and Indian—although with some apprehension. He may be ridiculed by his Indian family for marrying an African woman. Also, if a dougla person is raised in the African community, he or she is most likely to assume a Creole identity and develop little in-depth knowledge of the Indian side of the family. The opposite happens if the dougla person is raised in the Indian community. Paradoxically, a dougla person inherits at birth a bi-biological and bicultural world but experiences neither fully through life, primarily because of agnostic social relations between Africans and Indians.[4]

One of the questions generally associated with douglarization is whether or not it is a one-generation experience (Segal 1993). From a conservative biological perspective, it is only for one generation since further mixing would dilute biological aspects of douglarization—that is, the aspect of being 50 percent African and 50 percent Indian. However, the reality of douglarization is not grounded in only biological concepts, but it can be broadened to include cultural mixing in music such as Soca and Chutney. In an e-mail interview with Professor Patricia Moonsammy, a dougla, she writes that

douglarization, as a socio-cultural phenomenon, is subject to the politics that impact cultural processes. In periods leading up to and immediately following political elections, there is heightened entrenchment in the ethnically marked political camps of the two major political parties, the PNM [People's National Movement] and the UNC [United National Congress]. Despite the obvious ongoing douglarization through biological and cultural mixing, the discourse of opposition and polarization in politics and in the media is very apparent—in opinion pieces in print media, comments made by callers to talk radio, etc. However, Trinidad continues to be a small island where people live in close and intimate contact. There continues to be biological and cultural douglarization. My research reveals that the meaning of dougla is changing over time to index general mixedness, where Indian is part of the mix, rather than the historical notion of dougla as the mixture of a "pure" African and "pure" Indian. (2015)

While recognizing the contributions to as well as the diversity of Indian Caribbean identity, the purpose here is to provide alternative analyses of identity. The focus will be on Coolieology and on local, national, trans-Caribbean, and global identities.

COOLIEOLOGY

The word Coolie appears to have derived from Hindi *kuli* or from Tamil *kuli*, meaning wages. The use of the word in Indian communities toward low-wage laborers bore no negative connotation. The word became pejorative when Europeans began to transport Asian laborers to their overseas colonies to work on their tropical sugar plantations. The word became a permanent slur when Europeans used it during the period of indentureship in the nineteenth and twentieth centuries and when it was copied and used by other colonized ethnic groups during and after the above period. While the word was applied to low-wage Asian laborers, Chinese included, and even in the United States it became synonymous with Indian indentured laborers and their descendants in British colonies.

Over the years a number of literary scholars (Rajkumari Singh, Khal Torabully, and David Dabydeen) and a few writers (Guiatra Bahadur) have tried to destigmatize and desensitize the word, imbuing it with positive connotations. The first person to view the word positively was the distinguished Guyanese writer and leader Rajkumari Singh. She writes: "In return for our HERITAGE what greater tribute can we pay to them than to keep alive the name by which they were called COOLIE as a beautiful word that conjures up poignancy, tears, defeats and achievements. The word must not be left to die out, buried and forgotten in the past. It must be given a new lease of life" (1996, originally published in 1973; emphasis in original). She urges: "Proclaim the word! Identify with the word! Proudly say to the word 'I am a Coolie'" (1996). Since this plea, a number of emerging writers have taken the word and transformed it from a crude expletive to a concept with credibility. No other scholar has been more successful than Khal Torabully in moving the word forward, particularly in his ongoing analysis of Coolitude some twenty-five years after he developed the term. Torabully explains:

I also thought it was important to redefine this colonial slur, coolie, to make a new semantic and semiological appropriation of the word in a creative way. Indeed, why should we still suffer when people, sometimes, purposely use this word in an insulting or derogatory way? What would prevent us from re-appropriating it, as a kind of creative vision allowing us to be, as poets and semiologists, masters of language, capable of infusing new definitions in language, and not to be only the subaltern of the word/world, the indentured one who is always obliged

to carry the meanings the Other forged upon our memory and History.
(Roopnarine 2016, 289)

The word has certainly taken a new, positive dimension in the literary field.
However, it is argued here that the ideology and the negative reality of the
word still exist, which has caused the descendants of indentured Indians in
the Caribbean enormous pain. Those who use the word in scholarship or in
society reveal ignorance. The word Coolie is the most explosive word in the
Caribbean Indian experience. No other word has come close to having the
same ability to insult. This epithet belongs in a league of its own. Some use
it casually, especially among Indians themselves. Some use it defiantly, like
in St. Lucia and Jamaica. It is impossible to say the word without expanding
your mouth and showing your teeth. The word exists in other languages. The
word is spelled differently in different places but the poisonous meaning is
the same. The word has deep roots going back to the days of indenture, the
plantation prison. Consider the following epithet that has survived indenture, "pork and spice, Coolie watered rice." This epithet is not only used by
other ethnic groups but also by Indians. For instance, upper-class and urban
Indians when angry and frustrated with their children often accuse them of
acting like country Coolie. To people who have been poor ever since they
arrived in the Caribbean, tradition is what they have. The word disrupts this
tradition. The word enrages them.

    If there is any solace associated with this word it is that it is one of those
words that bind, and in some ways, it unifies the descendants of indentured
Indians around the globe. It reminds them of their sordid history and makes
them aware that they are still dragging the chains of indenture. They have not
emancipated themselves from indenture. They have yet to find a niche in the
Caribbean, despite having been in the region for over one hundred and fifty
years. To be sure, the word Coolie is not simply a word of abuse—demeaning and divisive. It is a word of endearment and empowerment. Take, for
example, a common expression among Indians: "Coolie bhai like he dhal
and rice, ah Coolie head hard, man." The word is used among rural Indians
in common speech to maintain camaraderie. However, the regular use of the
word has counterbalanced attempts to cast new images on it. The Band-Aid
approach to the word has not sufficed. There are two reasons for this. First,
the word has not been discussed enough for us to fully understand when
it should or should not be used. The attempt to put a positive spin on the
word is not only limited to the literary field, but it is also sketched in terms
of providing limited information. Second, the word is yet to be considered

hate speech or a racial slur, and therefore there is no disgrace in using it. There is no penalty. An Indian in the Caribbean, especially where he or she is in the minority, will certainly hear this: "Ernie menial money Moe, catch a Coolie and bit he toe."

ETHNO-LOCAL IDENTITY

Local Indian identity is a form of identity in which Indians have retained many of their ancestral or former homeland customs, particularly with regard to their attachment to ecology (land), religion (Hinduism and Islam), and extended family networks (Rauf 1974). This is noticeable mainly in some rural areas in the Caribbean where Indians have settled, such as in the Corentyne area of Guyana; Barrackpore, South Trinidad; and Nannie Polder, Suriname. Some pockets of local Indian identity also exist throughout the Caribbean, including urban areas. Local identity has developed and survived because of two fundamental factors. The first is that Indians were placed in isolated communities on the plantations during indenture. Subsequently, and even today, some Indian communities have made little contact with other ethnic groups, and therefore have not been influenced by other ethnic customs. Indian identity continued in tandem with their homeland culture with some internal modification. The second is that even when they came into contact with other ethnic groups, they held on to their homeland ways to protect themselves from assimilation into the wider Caribbean culture, creolization, and Christianization. This was very noticeable when Christian missionaries tried to convert Indians to Christianity. While a small percentage of Indians converted, a majority of them, with the guidance and influence of their Brahmin priests, resisted their language, religious beliefs, and the overall impact of Westernization on their children and community (see Samaroo 1982).

In modern times, local Indian identity has resisted being absorbed into the national culture of Guyana, Trinidad, and Suriname that is based on the axiom "all of us are one," which emphasizes Euro-Afro or Western characteristics. Writing for the *Guyana Times* newspaper, politician and religious leader Ravi Dev declares:

The question as to whether "unity" or "diversity" should be privileged is partially a semantic one, caused by the conflation of "state" and "nation." But at the bottom the dispute has to do with power as it almost

always does. Political unity and cultural diversity do not have to be
mutually exclusive. Each society has to find the right balance between
the demands of the two concepts that is appropriate for its own circumstances so as to have a political system that is cohesive and stable,
while facilitating the cultural aspirations of all the peoples. (2016)

Dev concludes: "We have proposed before, the creation of institutions to promote an ideological notion of 'Guyaneseness' for a nation based on equality,
which incorporates all our present cultures. Having one's social institutions
embody one's culture means that they will be immediately comprehensible
to us and therefore easier to use" (2016). Such a commentary emerged partly
from Guyana's dark period of dictatorship led by the predominately African
People's National Congress Party from 1966 to 1992. The government's restrictive economic substitution policy affected Indian material culture—food,
dress, and religious items. The government banned these imported items in
an attempt to encourage the use and consumption of local commodities.
However, some Indian items could not be substituted, and Indians saw the
government's policy as a direct attack on their culture. While they were not
totally against the regime, since they depended on it, the regime's restrictive
policy pushed Indians into a sort of localism in which they relied on their
internal communal support system to hold on to their local identity. Others
migrated to North America, but some reconstructed their local identity in
their new enclave.

The Indian local identity is based on an elastic form of Hinduism and
Islamic customs and is considered to be sacred and pure. It is used not only
to maintain aspects of custom and culture—Holi, Diwali, and Ramadan, for
example—but also to provide strong personal and communal support to
deal with socioeconomic problems such as alcoholism, suicide, and domestic aggression and abuse, particularly since these communities are generally without sound support networks. These communities have developed
survival mechanisms by themselves for themselves. Learning Hindi and
arranging marriages among Hindus are encouraged to maintain a sense
of *we*-ness or *we*-consciousness. Various nontraditional medical practices
coupled with folkloric beliefs from local Indian massage therapists such as
dealing with *nara* (belly pain), infertility, and abortion are very much evident
in Indian communities, which are not seen and recognized in other ethnic
communities (Mahabir 2011). Indian Muslims too have also displayed unique
ethno-local sentiments. Marriage customs like *mahr* (dowry), emphasis on
chastity before marriage, purdah, and preference for halal food have found

a formidable place among ethno-local Indian Muslims. Professor Halima-Sa'adi Kassim speculates that in rural Trinidad social interaction and social solidarity may display a closer attachment to the religion and practice of it and a higher affinity to the customs and traditions associated with being Muslim such as the five pillars of Islam (2016). These elements are crucial for the survival of local Indian identity since rural Indian communities are plagued by poverty, suicide, and other forms of dissonance.

Ethno-Indian local identity also reflects a sense of parochialism and insularity, which has given rise to internal and external problems. Internally, traditional roles within the family and community are questioned. Sons challenge the authority of fathers while daughters-in-law question their subservient roles in the family. Subsequently, effective social integration from the inside is not always strong as family, community, and society are torn apart by the struggle for power and equality. It is not uncommon to see family members not speaking to each other for long periods and in some cases a lifetime because of an argument. Indians themselves are separated and even torn apart by their different identifications. Some urban Indians simply despise local Indian identity and see it as backward and barnacled to old customs that are inconsistent with the more influential Creole identity. After the post-2015 general election in Guyana in which the predominant Indian People's Progressive Party (PPP) lost to the A Partnership for National Unity (APNU) and Alliance For Change (AFC) coalition, local Indians who retained their loyalty to the PPP were described as: "dem Coolie stupid," "dem Coolie na want change," "dem Coolie think dem a live in India."[5] What these remarks highlight is an internal ethnic identity difference within Indians in the Caribbean but more so in Guyana. While urban Indians have identified mainly with the national identity of their country, rural Indians with local identity see such aspirations as straying from one's roots. Rural Indians see themselves as proud icons of Indian cultural resilience in a foreign land, particularly with regard to rejecting Westernization and creolization. To be sure, however, some urban Indians as well as rural Indians embrace a hybrid identity that combines elements of both identities. It is not surprising to find an urban Hindu magistrate upholding Western law in courts or a rural Indian exposing his children to Western mannerisms and education.

Externally, Indian local identity is perceived by the Creole society as unsupportive of the national culture or national consciousness, which is based on nationality rather than ethnicity. As a result, Indian local identity can be marginalized from the national consciousness but at the local level shares an interlocking interdependence with communities different from the Indians' own. For instance, local Indians seek out Westernized Indians as well as Africans for help in matters relating to Western institutions such as schools and court proceedings. In some ways, and even though local Indian identity is insular, it is not always isolated. It can best be described as consensual, conflictual, and relational (Allahar 2004).

ETHNO-NATIONAL IDENTITY

A national identity is a form of identity whereby someone or a group of people expresses a feeling of attachment to a nation-state. This feeling may vary from casual to mild to intense. It may also be manufactured or manipulated, and individuals who embrace national identity tend to draw on some myths of the past to claim a secure place in the nation-state. To deal with the different expressions and approaches of nationalism, particularly in multiethnic states, governments tend to project or facilitate a common sense of belonging (nationalism). This process is called the nationalization of culture whereby a national culture, a mixture of all cultures, takes precedence over one particular culture. Governments, however, are careful to allow some degree of cultural autonomy during the process of the nationalization of culture.

In multicultural Guyana, Trinidad, and Suriname, much discussion has taken place about how various ethnic groups fit into the national culture. This discussion actually began in the 1960s when these countries were on the verge of achieving independence from their colonial masters (see Persad and Maharaj 1993). The main argument is that in moving forward these countries should not rely on but acknowledge their past, specifically their ancestral home, to define themselves. This is a convincing argument since Caribbean people have evolved tremendously since leaving their ancestral homeland. The problem, however, is that the Caribbean has evolved along Euro-African trends in government, education, and, to some extent, religion. Other ethnic groups who arrived during and after this evolution   a gradual departure from the past and a mixing of politics, cultures, and economics—and have retained some of their ancestral customs do not necessarily express their national identity like other ethnic groups. Jamaicans, for example, do not say they are African Jamaicans but Jamaicans, unless, of course, they are living in England or in North America. In these countries, they are pressed to declare or reveal their ethnicity and location mainly to disassociate themselves from other stigmatized African groups. By contrast, Indians in Guyana and

Suriname and less so Trinidad, if they are not politicized into creolization, generally tend to express an ethno-national identity or sub-ethno-national identity. That is, they express their feelings toward their home state alongside the ethnicity, customs, and languages that are specific to them—Bhojpuri, Sarnami, and Urdu languages and Eid al-Fitr, Bakra eid, and Muharram celebrations, for example—which may exclude other ethnic groups. When asked, for example, "Who are you?" the reply is, "I am an Indo-Trinidadian," or "an Indo-Surinamese," indicating that they recognize their cultural heritage or ethnicity alongside their national identity. They also link a sense of belonging, progress, and development with their dual identity. In Trinidad, for example, Muslims have pushed for their traditional headscarf—the hijab—to be worn in non-Muslim denominational schools (Kassim 2016).

While the expression of ethno-national identity may serve as a sense of place and camaraderie for Indians, especially when they are not in control of politics in Guyana, Trinidad, and Suriname, the mere idea of ethno-national identity has been controversial. To some, it demonstrates that Indians want to be separate from the national culture and they do not value and share Creole norms. Such sentiments reached a breaking point in Guyana in 2015 when an Indian politician declared that he was not an Indian but a Guyanese, implying that Guyana comes first and ethnicity later, if at all. A substantial number of Indians, particularly from the predominantly Indian opposition, were offended by the politician's remark, asking what sort of a message he was sending to the younger generation of Indians. One middle-aged Indian man said, "He is dismissing his ethnicity and culture. Have you seen any African politicians do that in Guyana? They are proud of being African."[6]

On another level, the quest for ethno-national identity in multiethnic Guyana, Trinidad, and Suriname can be problematic, leading to ethnic tensions. The jockeying for power along ethnic lines in these countries can result in hegemonic control and the exclusion of other ethnic groups in important sectors of society. Favoritism and competition for limited resources—jobs, housing, land, education, and credit—fuel discontent and civic strife, making these countries virtually ungovernable and trapped in a cycle of wasted opportunities. This is less so in Trinidad and Suriname than in Guyana. While no set repressive measures are implemented to suppress and make demands on ethnic groups, the perception is that the ethnic group that controls the levers of power tends to engage in witch hunting, removing members of the opposition party in important political posts.

Ethno-national identity does not have to be restricted to one's nation of birth. It can be expressed outside one's nation of birth in diasporic communities such as in North America. In these distant and different communities and countries Caribbean Indians find out very quickly upon arrival who they are. It is also in these environments that they are quick to declare and express their ethno-national identity. Until recently, all nonwhite persons were considered black. An average white person in the United States does not differentiate between black and brown people. To them, all nonwhite people are black. To some people, such as Caribbean Indians, the nonwhite-people's label is offensive. It is not that Caribbean Indians despise blacks—they have more in common with black Caribbeans than South Asians—but they do not want to be mislabeled and mistreated.

To demonstrate, in the United States and Canada, no category for Caribbean Indians exists in the census, so they are given the choice of identifying themselves as black West Indians or South Asians. Coming from an environment where race and ethnicity are more important to them than class, Caribbean Indians find being treated as blacks, South Asians, or Arabs to be demeaning and have strived to maintain an identity that suits them. The collective classification and subsequent identification of Caribbean Indians as something other than themselves misrepresents and undermines the unique differences among Caribbean people in North America. Ralph Premdas declares: "For Indo-Caribbean persons, their self-ascribed cultural particularity was rendered invisible by virtue of their being subsumed under a wider polyglot Caribbean identity. To be sure, on a day-to-day basis, they lived a separate and destructive cultural life even though they partly merged with diasporic Indian communities and re-invent their identity" (2004, 550). Added to this is the fact that Caribbean Indian persons are defensive if they are labeled as black West Indians or South Asians in North America and may go to great lengths to "educate" whites in small, immediate, and friendly circles about where they come from and who they are, even though they may have little meaningful contact with their former homeland. The very urge for a separate identity, however, may prevent Caribbean Indians from forming alliances with other ethnic groups to achieve greater goals such as racial equality in white societies (see Roopnarine 2009b).

TRANS-CARIBBEAN IDENTITY

An Indian trans-Caribbean identity is when an Indian does not identify or see him or herself in relation to a specific country in the Caribbean but identifies with belonging to other countries in the Caribbean. His thoughts, feelings, and behaviors are in line with those of other countries in the Caribbean. However, the countries of belonging share somewhat similar characteristics. For instance, Indians tend to share a trans-Caribbean identity with Guyana, Trinidad, and Suriname, countries with large Indian populations, rather than with Antigua, St. Kitts, Puerto Rico, or Cuba, which have few Indians and a different sense of identity.

Trans-Caribbean identity is not common among Indians, but it is an alternative form of identity that cannot be easily dismissed. This form of identity is religiously oriented in the form of Hinduism and Islam to provide a sense of security and stability for trans-Caribbean Indians. For Hindus, it is expressed through the assertive Indian Council for Cultural Relations (ICCR), Arya Samaj, and Santan Dharma. For Muslims, it is expressed through The Inter-Colonial Muslim Organization, Ahmadiyya organizations, Quranic recitation, and Qaseeda competitions (Kassim 2016). These sentiments are also expressed in Christian organizations and may comprise other ethnic groups like Africans in the Christian Baptist religion. These religious organizations have pushed for Indian empowerment, recognition, and revitalization in a creolized Caribbean (see Klass 1996 for the revitalization movement in Trinidad; Van der Veer and Vertovec 1991 for Brahmanism across the Caribbean). In Guyana, Trinidad, and Suriname, many Hindu and Islamic schools attract Indian students, teachers, pundits, and imams from these countries as well as from India, Pakistan, and the Middle East. Jap-A-Joe, Shie, and Vernooiji (2001) write that in Suriname "Hindus and Muslims have intensified and broadened external contacts, not only with India and Pakistan, but also with countries in the region—particularly Guyana and Trinidad—and with the Arabic world" (210).

Indian trans-Caribbean identity is not restricted to the insular Caribbean but it is also noticeable and vocal in the North American and European diaspora (see Gowricharn 2009 for the Netherlands). This is possible because, as Benedict Anderson (1991) suggests elsewhere, a trans-Caribbean identity can be imagined. Even though Indians in the diaspora have no personal knowledge of each other, they share a civic nation in which similar values, interests, images of camaraderie, citizenship, and community are expressed. It is in New York, Toronto, and London, for example, where the images of a civic trans-Caribbean identity are expressed. To feel connected with their trans-Caribbean identity in these new societies that discriminate, Indian Caribbean emigrants have formed associations like the Ontario Society for Services to the Indo-Caribbean Community (OSSICC) to deal with the everyday challenges of North American society and to practice segmented assimilation patterns, that is, maintaining contact with the Caribbean while integrating selectively into North American society. These Indians express a trans-Caribbean identity through their transnational lifestyle. They are in Canada, for example, but their Caribbean past is highlighted, their achievements in Canada are appreciated, and their differences from Canadians are valued. Some of this is expressed in associations, churches, clubs, newspapers, and radio stations. For some, a search for or an expression of trans-Caribbean identity is genuine, while for others it is an excuse for claims and counter-claims in a foreign land. One critic declares that this form of identity is not unusual because it represents a quest for unity "in a fragmented and fractured world" in which the Caribbean is at the forefront (Premdas 1995, 77).

ETHNO-INDIAN UNIVERSAL IDENTITY

Like so many other ethnic groups around the world, globalization has also shaped Caribbean Indian identity. Globalization has had a double impact on Caribbean Indian people; that is, it has brought them closer socially and economically but has also driven them apart, undermining their institutions and traditional ways of life. Despite this, a gradual formation of Indian universal identity has emerged, which is separate from other forms of Caribbean identity. An Indian universal identity is not restricted to local, national, and regional locations but it is a combination of these locations, which makes it universal. Whenever and wherever Indians have resided, they do not necessarily see themselves belonging to that particular geographical space—local, national, or regional. Instead, their identity is linked to other Indian communities around the world. In this drive for a universal sense of belonging, Indians may not share the same characteristics, particularly with regard to the retention of Indian customs and assimilation into Western values.

Indian universal identity has been shaped overwhelmingly by the forces of migration. The first occurred during the period of European colonialism in the nineteenth and early twentieth centuries. An estimated two million Indians were taken out of India to provide indentured labor in former European slave colonies in the Indian Ocean and Pacific islands, Asia, South Africa, and the Caribbean. An estimated one-third of these indentured laborers returned to India, but the remainder of them stayed in their respective colonies as permanent settlers. The second migration is more contemporary, starting soon after the Second World War and after India achieved independence in 1947. An estimated twenty million Indians have migrated out of

India since this period and have settled mainly in Europe, North America, Australia, and the Middle East. These are mainly skilled Indians. These two migrations have certainly caused an Indian diaspora, with some depth of interconnectedness through business and religion.

Since the 1950s there has been a concerted effort to connect India with the "Indian Caribbean." Indian missionaries or Swamis and Imams from India have lived in Indian Caribbean communities preaching and teaching Hindu and Islamic spirituality. Likewise, Indian Caribbean religious leaders have often traveled to the Indian subcontinent and the Arab world for wider knowledge and inspiration to share with their respective communities upon return. Sentiments of closer connection between the above locations and the Caribbean are expressed through individual lectures, associations, and media. To illustrate, January 9, the day Mahatma Gandhi returned from South Africa in 1910, is considered to be Pravasi Bharatiya Divas, meaning "people of Indian origin day," a rainbow with many hues. A yearly conference is also held around January 9, and Indians from the diaspora attend and present papers relating to Indian issues. During some of these yearly conferences, Indian leaders like Bharrat Jagdeo and Basdeo Panday were recipients of achievement awards. It was also revealed in one conference that the Indian government has granted dual citizenship to sixteen countries in the diaspora with India populations. The reason for dual citizenship is to renew bonds that were lost by separation and to reestablish cultural and spiritual links with the diaspora and India. The Indian government declares that all Indians constitute the global Indian family, and efforts are skewed in that direction to promote universal blood brother and sisterhood, especially in former indentured communities, where there exists a widespread nostalgia for India.

To facilitate a Caribbean Indian connection with India and the Arab world, travel agencies offer special deals in the Caribbean as well as in North America. Indian films (Bollywood) and music continue to pour into the Indian diaspora. Several symposia and seminars have been organized. The University of the West Indies in Trinidad has organized Indian Diaspora Conferences in 1975, 1984, 2004, 2005, 2012, and 2015. There is also a Center for the Study of Indian Diaspora at the University of Hyderabad in India. The Global Organization of People of Indian Origin (GOPIO) has been vocal in expressing the need for a universal Indian identity, among other things, during its annual conference. The ultimate motive behind these conferences is to engage the diaspora with mother India on issues that affect overseas Indians, such as ethnic discrimination, ethnic conflict, ethnic identity and culture, and business opportunities.

There are also noticeable Muslim connections in Guyana, Trinidad, and Suriname with international Muslim organizations. Guyana and Suriname are members of the Organization of Islamic Cooperation (OIC), which is an intergovernmental organization and is seen as the collective voice of the Muslim world, which works to safeguard and protect the interests of the Muslim world in the spirit of promoting international peace and harmony among various people of the world.[7]

In summary, Indian global identity is shaped by Indians whose histories have been affected by forces beyond their control. Their identity has been shaped more by global experience and less by one specific geographic location. Their sense of belonging is not tied to a nation-state but to the larger universal community that shares their values and norms.

CONCLUSION

The aim of this book was to analyze the migration and identity formation of people of South Indian descent in the Caribbean, principally in Guyana, Trinidad, and Suriname, as well as in the Indian diaspora in Western Europe (Britain and the Netherlands) and North America (the United States and Canada). The findings and assessments can be divided into four distinct but interconnected points.

First, of all Indian migrations, the movement from India to the Caribbean has received the most attention, mainly from a historical perspective. The reason for this is that the movement from India to the Caribbean was the longest continuous (eighty years out of 176) Indian migration since they settled in the Caribbean. Moreover, this migration attracted more attention because of the ambiguities surrounding it. The descendants, including academics and researchers, are not sure about intricacies of this indentured migration, although there seems now to be a fair understanding of this aspect of Indian migration. What appeared alongside this understanding, however, are some shortcomings in the literature of this indentured migration. There has been a repetition of information, namely that Indians migrated because of push and pull factors. This book acknowledges this argument but goes further and takes the position that Indians also migrated because of an expansion of world capitalism and the program of imperialism and colonialism. A majority of them did not have a fair understanding of where they were going, so they conjured up their own projections of the unknown, which provided a psychological help to their long migratory journey. The reality of the journey, especially the internal movement to the depot, the depot itself, and the sea crossing, taxed and tested their physiological and psychological strength. A majority survived, but they would never be the same again. Initially, they tried to retain their differences, but over time they realized that it was a futile ambition. Instead, they put aside differences and bonded together and formed makeshift families that produced a subculture for internal support and protection from predation. This social strategy did not eliminate abuse but provided a safety valve for indentured Indians, which they took with them not only throughout their indentured lives but shared with future generations of indentured laborers. This was noticeable during and beyond indenture when they created innovative ways to migrate and improve their lives through desertion and legal action. What resulted from this initiative and development was the formation of a vibrant Indian community and peasantry around plantations, which is still very much present in Guyana. Indians reconstructed their culture and attachment to ecology and engaged in sugar and rice cultivation and cattle rearing. An Indian elite class as well as a working class emerged within the Indian communities that paralleled the larger plantation system of dominant white plantation owners.

The acquisition of a rural-urban culture in terms of acquiring a higher education and becoming more Westernized also occurred. Indian children in rural areas began to move to urban areas to acquire better-paying jobs and greater opportunities. This dispersal of Indians from their rural base caused them to become more visible in all sectors of Guyana's, Trinidad's, and Suriname's society. This pattern has continued into the present. There is little doubt that indentured Indians benefitted from their indenture contracts, but this cannot always be measured by how much they saved and remitted back to India. An exposure to a different way of life, despite its oppressiveness, certainly had an impact on their lives forever. The opportunity to have choices, in regard to juxtaposing life in India and the Caribbean, was perhaps the most compelling reason for staying in the Caribbean or returning to India.

Secondly, the modern Caribbean migration after the 1930s to within the Caribbean and Europe and North America was inspired by the need for religious cultural connection, economic opportunities, and proximity of Indian communities in the Southern Caribbean as well as by political turbulence, ethnic tensions in the Caribbean, and various immigration policies established under CARICOM. Indians who migrated to these destinations have had a paradoxical experience: they have blended comfortably in some islands, like in Trinidad, but have faced greater challenges of acceptance and integration in other islands, like in Barbados. The movement to Europe and North America has shown similar patterns, although with some notable differences. This movement has received the most attention primarily because of its visibility and enormous impact on the sending and receiving territories. This movement has occurred in tandem with global inequities in the modern nation system and reformed immigration laws as well as political, economic, and social instabilities in the Caribbean. The movement has really been insular, from one colonial territory to the mother country. For example, Indo-Surinamese generally migrate to the Netherlands. This extra-regional migration began slowly and selectively, attracting mainly the educated class. By the 1980s, this migration had become full blown, attracting Indo-Caribbeans from all strata of Caribbean society, to the point where an estimated half of the Indian Caribbean population of Guyana, Trinidad, and Suriname now reside in developed countries. They have faced bouts of racism, marginalization, social tensions, anxiety, and depression amid gradual success. The second generation of Indians, however, has shown a more broad-based participation and has subsequently made more significant inroads in developed countries. They are involved in government, education, and business rather than being restricted to the working-class environment like the first-generation migrants. Much of this success has to do with inspiration and awareness of opportunities among second-generation Indian citizens coupled with steady support from their first-generation families and communities. One of the most distinctive commonalities among Indians in the European and North American diasporas is that a majority do not have the desire to return home, but they will visit occasionally. They also contribute to their departed homeland via remittances. Notable also is that The Netherlands has been more proactive in the integration process (for example, offering subsided housing) of Caribbean Indians while North American countries have not gone out of their way to help Caribbean Indians. These migrants have to fend for themselves through various self-made and self-developed organizations and associations in the drive to understand the complexities and opportunities in developed countries. They are now more active in asserting their new space but at the same time are losing some of their homeland ways, coupled with the emerging trend of a secondary internal migration from the original Indian diaspora communities to other communities. Some Indians have ended up living in communities in which there are very few commonalities, but they are willing to adjust to their new environment. Other Indians have moved into societies with smaller Indian populations and have joined in the process of rebuilding themselves and their communities as they had done in their original diasporic society. The difference between the first migration and the second internal migration is that the latter is less difficult since the migrants have acquired some experience with the host society prior to migrating. Actually, the experience with their original base has encouraged them to explore new and broader opportunities. The final pattern of Indian migration during the modern period replicates the first Indian migration, albeit in different forms. There has been a steady migration of Indians from India called NRIs, or non-resident Indians, in the Caribbean. Although this movement originates from India—and that in some ways bring the Indian migration full circle, in that it started from India in the nineteenth century and returned to India today—this current migration is unrelated to indentured migration. This migration is made up of a professional class of Indians: diploma holders, doctors, teachers, businesspeople, and religious migrants. It is the only group of Indians within the overall Indian migration that has moved with some secure financial resources. Their movement can be classified as moving from a more- to a less-advanced environment with the ultimate aim of investing and growing in the latter environment. They have been very successful in this regard, at least materially, and, in some ways, in cultural reconstruction. Unlike a majority of the descendants of indentured Indians who reside around the challenging plantation domains, these NRIs live a privileged and prestigious life. Their residences are located in well-to-do neighborhoods and their children attend the best schools in the host country and even overseas, including India. These recent NRIs see themselves as immigrants first and residents second, and, subsequently, have little meaningful contact with the wider society other than their oc-cupational connections and Indian-related activities. Some NRIs express a deep admiration toward Trinidadian Indians for holding on to their past Indian culture, something NRIs have taken for granted.

Third, in spite of the drive toward globalization, some sections of the Indian population, mostly in rural areas, have retained impressive levels of ethno-localization. What this means is that Indians have retained many of their ancestral or former homeland customs, particularly with regard to their attachment to ecology (land), religion (Hinduism and Islam), and extended family networks. Some areas in which this ethno-localization has occurred are Corentyne, Guyana; Barrackpore, South Trinidad; and Nannie Polder, Suriname. Some pockets of local Indian identity also exist throughout the Caribbean, including in urban areas. Likewise, Indians have assumed an ethno-national identity that is much broader than an ethno-local identity, expressing feelings of attachment to a nation-state based on ethnicity and nationalism. What may arise from this ethno-national position is the percep-tion that Indians want to be separate from the national culture, generating a feeling of ethnic insecurity. There exists also an ethno-trans-Caribbean identity among Indians whereby the sense of belonging and feeling of homeland is not restricted to one Caribbean country but is connected to other Caribbean countries with significant Indian populations. This identity is religiously oriented in the form of Hinduism and Islam and less so around Christianity, but it exists primarily to provide a sense of security and stability for trans-Caribbean Indians. Like ethno-national identity, an ethno-trans-Caribbean identity is expressed imaginatively outside of the Caribbean such as in the European and North American diasporas. This form of identity exists in foreign lands to deal with the throes of departure from one's homeland as well as the challenges associated with effective and efficient integration in developed society. The final ethno-global identity of Indians has been the least recognized but is the most connected of the multipartite forms of identity because of globalization, which arguably has brought Indians, wherever they are, closer to each other. An ethno-global Indian universal identity is not expressed and restricted to local, national, and regional locations, but it is a combination of these locations.

Fourth, predicting the future is always a risky endeavor, but if we analyze some predominant patterns in the past and in the modern period we can make some safe speculations. Caribbean Indians will continue to migrate because of inequities in the global system as well as political, economic, and social instabilities and tensions within each nation-state where Indians have migrated and settled—Guyana, Trinidad, Suriname, and in the European and North American diasporas. Migration will also continue because a culture of migration has now formed among Indians that is predicated on the belief that in order to grow and develop one has to migrate, despite how temporally. Half of the Indian population in Guyana and Suriname live outside of these countries. What will also happen in the future is that certain patterns of migration will dominate. The preferred destination will be to developed countries and less so within the Caribbean, particularly among Indo-Trinidadians, reflecting a hierarchy of migration. Vertical rather than horizontal forms of migration will be the preferences. The latter will occur when the first preference is denied, particularly among economically deprived Indo-Guyanese who tend to migrate almost anywhere in the Caribbean. Some trends of migration will continue. Outward rather than inward migration will continue, meaning that when Indians leave their respective homeland only a minority of them will return, even occasionally. The new diasporic communities will be the preferred places to live because of attachment, investment, and the second and third generations who have very little knowledge of the first-generation lifestyle in their departed homeland. It is also predicted that sentiments of and remittances to homeland will be progressively reduced. Nonetheless, Caribbean Indian migrants will continue to shape their departed and new destinations. The sending countries will lose skilled and educated Indians and receiving countries will obviously benefit from them. Political parties in the Caribbean will continue more rigorously to court overseas Indians to contribute to their election to office. Interesting, too, will be the continued perception that Indians are better off in developed countries than in the Caribbean, despite the racism, marginalization, loneliness, loss of culture, and unfavorable climate in developed countries. The future of Indian identity is more challenging to predict. The four multipartite models offered in this book will certainly change and ethno-local identity may disappear altogether like in other localized cultures because of globalization. Ethno-national identity will continue because it is analogous with the existence of the nation-state. As long as Guyana, for example, exists, so will ethno-national identity because Indians will continue to identify with ethnicity first and national consciousness second, particularly if politicians continue to campaign for power based on ethnic lines. The universal or global identity of Indians will become stronger in terms of awareness but less coordinated because of the dispersal of Indians within the global system.

NOTES

INTRODUCTION

1. See the proceedings of the Indentured Labor Route International Conference in Mauritius, November 2–5, 2014; the 150th anniversary of the abolition of Slavery and Indenture conference, Suriname, June 6, 2013; the International East Indian Diaspora Conference: East Indians in the Caribbean: Reflections of the Past; Charting the Way Forward, University of the West Indies, Trinidad, May 28–29, 2005; and the Globalization, Diaspora and Identity Formation conference, Paramaribo, Suriname, February 26–29, 2004.

CHAPTER FOUR: INDIAN MIGRATION WITHIN THE CARIBBEAN

1. Author's field notes, Upper Corentyne, Guyana, July 2015.
2. Ibid.
3. Ibid., August 2015.
4. Author's field notes, New Nickerie, Suriname, August 2015.
5. Ibid.
6. Ibid.
7. Ibid.
8. See the United Nations Development Programme's Human Development Reports, http://hdr.undp.org/en/.
9. Interview with an Indo-Trinidadian in Port-of-Spain, Trinidad, May 16, 2015.
10. See www.coha.org/barbadia-first-policy-flogs-guyanese-in-barbados.
11. Interview with Indians at the Hindu temple on St. Croix, US Virgin Islands, October 2011.

CHAPTER FIVE: INDIAN MIGRATION FROM THE CARIBBEAN TO EUROPE AND NORTH AMERICA

1. Interview with an elderly Guyanese Indian woman in Syracuse, New York, June 22, 2014.
2. Interview with a former illegal alien in New York, June 12, 2012.
3. Interview with an Indo-Guyanese male in Queens, New York, May 15, 2013.

4. Interview with an Indo-Surinamese male in Jersey City, New Jersey, August 2, 2015.
5. Interview with an Indo-Guyanese male in Queens, New York, July 12, 2015.
6. Interview with an Indo-Guyanese male in Queens, New York, July 13, 2015.

CHAPTER SIX: NONINDENTURED INDIAN MIGRATION TO THE CARIBBEAN SINCE WORLD WAR II

1. Author's field notes, New Nickerie, Suriname, July 25, 2015.
2. See, for example, www.hcigeorgetown.org.
3. Author's field notes, Port of Spain, Trinidad, May 2015.
4. "United States Virgin Islands 2010 Census," U.S. Virgin Islands Demographic Files, Eastern Caribbean Center, University of the Virgin Islands, 2010.
5. Author's field notes, St. Croix, US Virgin Islands, fall 2009 and spring 2010.

CHAPTER SEVEN: INDIAN IDENTITY IN THE CARIBBEAN

1. Author's field notes, Berbice, Guyana, August 2, 2015.
2. Author's field notes, Upper Corentyne, Guyana, June 20, 2014.
3. Author's field notes, Upper Corentyne, Guyana, May 15, 2013.
4. For in-depth analyses on douglas in Trinidad, for example, see the studies by Eve Stoddard and Grant Cornwell (2001) and Aisha Khan (1993).
5. Author's field notes, Berbice, Guyana, July 2015.
6. Author's field notes, Upper Corentyne, Guyana, August 2015.
7. See www.oic-oci.org/page/?p_id=52&p_ref=26&lan=en.

REFERENCES

NOTES ON THE PRIMARY SOURCES

For the chapters on the migration of Indians from India to the Caribbean, from the Caribbean back to India, and the internal migration during indenture I have used primary archival information from archives in London, England; Georgetown, Guyana; and Port of Spain, Trinidad. For chapters on migration after indenture, I have conducted field research in Guyana, Trinidad, Suriname, and St. Croix in the US Virgin Islands. I have conducted field research in Queens, New York, and Jersey City, New Jersey, and to some extent in Canada, places with overseas Indian populations. I have also conducted e-mail interviews. The identities of interviewees cited in the text are concealed unless the interviewees agreed to have their names published.

Ali, Arif. 2015. Telephone interview. London, November 15.

Allahar, Anton, L. 2004. "Ethnic Entrepreneurship and Nationalism in Trinidad: Afrocentrism and Hindutva." *Social and Economic Studies* 53 (2): 117–54.

Amersfoort, Hans van. 2011. *How the Dutch Government Stimulated the Unwanted Immigration from Suriname.* IMI Working Papers Series 2011, No. 47. University of Oxford: International Migration Institute.

Anderson, Benedict. 1991. *Imagined Communities.* London: Verso Publications.

Bacchus, M. K. 1989. "Education and East Indians in Guyana." In *Indenture and Exile: The Indo-Caribbean Experience,* edited by Frank Birbalsingh, 171–75. Toronto: Tsar.

Bal, Ellen. 2012. *Country Report: Indian Migration to the Netherlands.* European University Institute: Robert Schuman Centre for Advanced Studies.

"'Barbados First' Policy Flogs Guyanese in Barbados." 2009. *Council on Hemisphere Affairs,* August 5. www.coha.org/barbadia-first-policy-flogs-guyanese-in-barbados.

Barros, De Juanita. 1997. "To Milk or Not to Milk?: Regulation of the Milk Industry in Colonial Georgetown." *Journal of Caribbean History* 1–2: 185–208.

Basham, A. L. 1964. *Studies in Indian History and Culture.* Calcutta: Sambodhi.

Bayly, Susan. 1999. *Caste, Society and Politics in India from the Eighteenth Century to the Modern Age*. Vol. 3 of *The New Cambridge History of India*. Cambridge: Cambridge University Press.

Bedminster, Eunice. 2005. "India Association Launches Local Fund Drive to Assist Tsunami Victims." *Virgin Islands Daily News*, January 3.

Berger, Joseph. 2014. "Indian, Twice Removed." *New York Times*, December 17.

Botwick, Charles. 2008. "India's Independence Marked by Gifts, Cultural Spice." *Virgin Islands Daily News*. August 24.

Brereton, Bridget. 1993. "Social Organization and Class, Racial and Cultural Conflict in Nineteenth Century Trinidad." In *Trinidad Ethnicity*, edited by Kevin Yelvington, 33–55. Knoxville: University of Tennessee Press.

Brijmohan, Nirmal. 2016. "Hindustani Elderly in the Netherlands." In *Social and Cultural Dimensions of Indian Indentured Labour and Its Diaspora: Past and Present*, edited by Maurits S. Hassankhan, Lomarsh Roopnarine, and Radica Mahase, 149–78. New Delhi: Manohar.

British Guiana. 1881. "Immigration Agent General (IAG) Report of the Immigration Agent General for the year 1880." In *The Argosy*. Georgetown, Guyana: Demerara.

———. 1882. "Immigration Agent General (IAG) Report of the Immigration Agent General for the year 1881." In *The Argosy*. Georgetown, Guyana: Demerara.

———. 1888. "Immigration Agent General (IAG) Report of the Immigration Agent General for the Year 1877." In *The Argosy*. Georgetown, Guyana: Demara.

———. 1907. "Immigration Agent General (IAG) Report of the Immigration Agent General for the year 1906." In *The Argosy*. Georgetown, Guyana: Demerara.

———. 1908. "Immigration Agent General (IAG) Report of the Immigration Agent General for the year 1907." In *The Argosy*. Georgetown, Guyana: Demerara.

———. 1909. "Immigration Agent General (IAG) Report of the Immigration Agent General for the year 1908." In *The Argosy*. Georgetown, Guyana: Demerara.

———. 1923. "Immigration Agent General (IAG) Report of the Immigration Agent General for the year 1922." In *The Argosy*. Georgetown, Guyana: Demerara.

———. 1930. "Immigration Agent General (IAG) Report of the Immigration Agent General for the year 1929." In *The Argosy*. Georgetown, Guyana: Demerara.

British Parliamentary Papers. 1837–38a. "Copy of Letter from John Gladstone, Esq. to Messrs. Gillanders, Arbuthnot & Co." (LII, 180). London: Colonial Record Office.

———. 1837–38b. "Copy of Letter from Messrs. Gillanders, Arbuthnot & Co. to John Gladstone, Esq." (LII, 232). London: Colonial Record Office.

———. 1862. *The Twenty-second General Report of the Colonial Land and Emigration Commissioners*. London: Irish University Press.

———. 1866. *The Twenty-sixth General Report of the Colonial Land and Emigration Commissioners*. London: Irish University Press.

———. 1871. *Report of the Commissioners appointed to Enquire into the Treatment of Immigrants in British Guiana*. Vol. 20 (C.393). London: Colonial Record Office.

———. 1874. *Report by Geoghegan on Immigration from India*. Vol. 47 (C314). London: Colonial Record Office.

———. 1904. *Coolie Immigration: Immigration Ordinance of Trinidad and British Guiana.* (Cd 1989). London: HMSO.

———. 1910a. *Report of the Committee on Emigration from India to the Crown Colonies and Protectorates (Sanderson Commission).* Vol. 27, part 1 (Cd. 5192–94). London: HMSO.

———. 1910b. "Testimony of Mr. Oliver Warner, Minutes of Evidence." In *Report of the Committee on Emigration from India to the Crown Colonies and Protectorates (Sanderson Commission).* Vol. 27, part 2 (Cd. 5192–94), para. 714. London: HMSO.

———.1910c. "Testimony of Sir Neville Lubbock, Minutes of Evidence." In *Report of the Committee on Emigration from India to the Crown Colonies and Protectorates (Sanderson Commission).* Vol. 27, part 2 (Cd. 5192–94), 94. London: HMSO.

———. 1915. *Report on the Condition of Indian Immigration in the four British Colonies (Trinidad, British Guiana or Demerara, Jamaica and Fiji) and in the Dutch Colony of Suriname or Dutch Guiana (McNeill-Lal Report).* Vol. 47 (Cd. 7744). London: HMSO.

Carter, Marina, and Khal Torabully. 2002. *Coolitude: An Anthology of Indian Labor Diaspora.* London: Anthem Press.

Choenni, Chan. 2011. "Integration Hindustani Style? On Migration, History and Diaspora of Hindustanis." Inaugural lecture delivered upon the acceptance of the Endowed Chair, Lalla Rookh, of Hindustani migration, Vrije Universiteit, Amsterdam, June 6, 2011.

———. 2013. "Happy in Holland: The Hindostani Elders in the Netherlands." *Sociological Bulletin* 62 (1): 40–58.

Clarke, Colin. 1967. "Caste among Hindus in a Town in San Fernando." In *Caste in Overseas Indian Communities,* edited by Barton M. Schwartz, 165–99. San Francisco: Chandler.

Clement, Richard, Sonia S. Singh, and Sophie Gaudet. 2006. "Identity and Adaptation among Minority Indo-Guyanese: Influence of Generational Status, Gender, Reference and Group and Situation." *Group Processes & Intergroup Relations* (GPIR) 9 (2): 289–304.

Comins, D. W. D. 1893a. *Notes on Emigration from India to British Guiana.* Calcutta: Bengal Secretariat.

———. 1893b. *Notes on Emigration from India to British Guiana, Trinidad, St. Lucia and on Return Passage.* Calcutta: Bengal Secretariat.

———. 1893c. *Notes on Emigration from India to Trinidad.* Calcutta: Bengal Secretariat.

"Connecting with Suriname, Guyana through Diaspora." 2015. *Times of India,* February 8. http://timesofindia.indiatimes.com/nri/other-news/Connecting-with-Suriname-Guyana-through-diaspora/articleshow/46166433.cms.

Cooper, Constance, and Sean McCoy. 2010. "Haiti Effort Gets Big Lift from India Association." *Virgin Islands Daily News,* February 9.

Dabydeen, David, and Brinsley Samaroo, eds. 1987. *India in the Caribbean.* London: Hansib.

Davids, Leo. 1964. "The East Indian Family Overseas." *Social and Economic Studies* 13: 383–96.

Degia, Haajim. 2007. "Ethnic Minority Dominance in a Small-Island Developing State and the Implications for Development: The Case of Barbados." Master's thesis, Ohio University.

Despres, Leo A. 1968. "Anthropology, Cultural Pluralism and the Study of Complex Societies." *Cultural Anthropology* 9 (1): 3–26.

Dev, Ravi. 2016. "Culture and Unity." *Guyana Times*, January 8.

"The Distribution of Indians on Danish St. Croix." 1863. *Coolie Journal*. Rigstarkivet, West Indike Lokalarkiver, Den Vest Indiske Regering: Danish National Archives.

Eriksen, Thomas. 1992. "Indians in the New World: Mauritius and Trinidad." *Social & Economic Studies* 41 (1): 157–87.

Fields, Tim. 2008. "India Association Celebrating Ancestral Homeland's Independence." *Virgin Islands Daily News*, August 22.

Focus Migration: Country Profile The Netherlands. 2007. Hamburg: Hamburg Institute of International Economics (HWWI).

Foucault, Michel. 1972. *The Archaeology of Knowledge*. Translated by A. M. Sheridan Smith. New York: Pantheon Books.

Garcia, F. I. 2004. "Demographic and Social Structural Changes in the Contemporary Caribbean." In *General History of the Caribbean*. Vol. 5, edited by Bridget Brereton, 410–33. London: UNESCO.

Gordijn, W., ed. 1977. *Encyclopedie van Suriname*. Amsterdam: Elsevier.

Gowricharn, Ruben. 2009. "Changing Forms of Transnationalism." *Ethnic and Racial Studies* 32 (9): 1619–38.

———. 2015. "Sociability Networks of Migrant Youngsters: The Case of Dutch Hindustanis." *Current Sociology* (September 29): 1–18. doi:10.1177/0011392115605628.

Grierson, George A. 1883. *Report on Colonial Emigration from Bengal Presidency*. Calcutta: Bengal Secretariat.

"Guyana Census." 2002. *Guyana.gov*. Accessed March 12, 2016. www.statisticsguyana.gov.gy/cen02.html.

"Guyanese in Barbados Being 'Stereotyped' on Basis of Appearance—Faria." 2009. *Stabroek News*, May 18. www.stabroeknews.com/2009/archives/05/18/guyanese-in-barbados-being-%E2%80%98stereotyped%E2%80%99-on-basis-of-appearance-%E2%80%93-faria.

Hanoomansingh, Peter. 1996. "Beyond Profit and Capital: A Study of the Sindhis and Gujaratis of Barbados." In *Ethnic Minorities in Caribbean Society*, edited by Rhoda Reddock, 273–342. Trinidad: Zenth Services Limited.

Hassankhan, Maurits. 2011. "Kahe gaile bides–Why Did You Go Overseas: An Emotional Aspect of Migration in a Diaspora Perspective." Paper presented at The Global South: Asian Diaspora in the 21st Century: Antecedents and Prospects conference. St. Augustine, Trinidad, University of the West Indies, June 1–14.

———. 2015. E-mail interview with author. Suriname, April 6.

Hoefte, Rosemarijn. 1998. *In Place of Slavery: A Social History of British Indian and Javanese Laborers in Suriname*. Gainesville: University Press of Florida.

Hosler, Akiko S., David S. Pratt, Kathryn A. Sen, Erin M. Buckenmeyer, Alexander Simao Jr., Ephraim E. Back, Sanghamitra Savadatti, Jennifer L. Kahn, and Glynnis S. Hunt. 2013. "High Prevalence of Diabetes among Indo-Guyanese Adults, Schenectady, New York." *Preventing Chronic Disease* 10. www.ncbi.nlm.nih.gov/pubmed/23537517.

"India Pledges Support to Help Guyana." 2016. *Guyana Chronicle*, January 27. http://guyanachronicle.com/india-pledges-support-to-help-develop-guyana.

Jap-A-Joe, H., P. S. Shie, and J. Vernooiji. 2001. "The Quest for Respect: Religion and Emancipation in Twentieth Century Suriname" In *20th Century Suriname: Continuities and Discontinuities in a New World Society*, edited by Rosemaijn Hoefte and Peter Meel, 198–219. Leiden, Neth.: KITLV.

Kassim, Hilma Sa'adi. 2016. E-mail exchange with author. Trinidad, December 12.

Kershaw, Sarah. 2002. "For Schenectady, a Guyanese Strategy; Mayor Goes All Out to Encourage a Wave of Hardworking Immigrants." *New York Times*, July 26.

Khan, Aisha. 1993. "What Is a 'Spanish': Ambiguity and 'Mixed' Ethnicity in Trinidad." In *Trinidad Ethnicity*, edited by Kevin Yelvington, 180–207. Knoxville: University of Tennessee Press.

Klass, Morton. 1961. *East Indians in Trinidad: A Study of Cultural Persistence*. New York: Columbia University Press.

———. 1996. *Singing with Sai Baba: The Politics of Revitalization in Trinidad*. Prospect Heights, IL: Waveland Press.

Laurence, Keith. 1994. *A Question of Labor: Indentured Immigration into Trinidad and British Guiana, 1875–1917*. New York: St Martin's Press.

Lewin, Aldeth. 2011. "Gross Receipts Tax Tops Business Concerns." *Virgin Islands Daily News*, July 14.

Look Lai, Walton. 1993. *Indentured Labor, Caribbean Sugar: Chinese and Indian Migrants to the British West Indies, 1838–1917*. Baltimore: The John Hopkins University Press.

Mahabir, Joy. 2015. E-mail interview with author. Queens, NY, May 4.

Mahabir, Kumar. 2011. "Women as Invisible Healers: Traditional Midwives in Trinidad and Tobago." In *Bindi: The Multifaceted Lives of Indo-Caribbean Women*, edited by Rosanne Kanhai, 165–79. Kingston: University of the West Indies Press.

Mahase, Radica. 2008. "Plenty a Dem Run Away: Resistance by Indian Indentured Labourers in Trinidad, 1870–1920." *Labor History* 49 (4): 465–80.

Malik, Yogendra K. 1971. *East Indians in Trinidad*. London: Oxford University Press.

Mansingh, Lakshmi, and Ajai Mansingh. 2000. *Home Away from Home: 150 Years of Indian Presence in Jamaica, 1845–1995*. Kingston, Jamaica: Ian Randle.

Manuel, Peter. 2015. *Tales, Tunes, and Tassa Drums: Retention and Invention in Indo-Caribbean Music*. Urbana: University of Illinois Press.

Marmaro, L. 1990. "Human Rights and Migration Policies." *Revista de la OIM sobre migraciones America Latina* 8 (2–3): 7–32.

Mishra, Sudesh. 2012. "'Bending Closer to the Ground': Girmit as Minor History." *Australian Humanities Review* (52, May). www.australianhumanitiesreview.org/archive/Issue-May-2012/mishra_s.html.

Mohan, Raj. 2008. *Bapauti. Erfenis (Bapauti-Legacy)*. Haarlem, Neth.: In de Knipscheer.

Mohapatra, Prabhu P. 1995. "Restoring the Family: Wife Murders and the Making of a Sexual Contract for Indian Immigrant Labor in the British Caribbean Colonies, 1860–1920." *Studies in History* 11 (2): 228–60.

Moonsammy, Patricia. 2015. E-mail interview with author. Port-of-Spain, Trinidad, November 20.

Moutoussamy, E. 1989. "Indianess in the French West Indies." In *Indenture and Exile: The Indo-Caribbean Experience*, edited by Frank Birbalsingh, 26–36. Toronto: Tsar.

Munasinghe, Viranjini. 2001. *Callaloo or Tossed Salad?: East Indians and the Cultural Politics of Identity in Trinidad*. Ithaca, NY: Cornell University Press.

Nakhuda, Sabir. 2013. *Bengal to Barbados: A 100 Year History of East Indians in Barbados*. Barbados: self-published.

Nevadomsky, Joseph. 1980a. "Changes in Hindu Institutions in an Alien Environment." *Eastern Anthropologist* 33 (1): 39–53.

———. 1980b. "Changes over Time and Space in the East Indian Family in Rural Trinidad." *Journal of Comparative Family Studies* 11 (4): 434–36.

Niehoff, Arthur, and Jaunita Niehoff. 1960. *East Indians in the West Indies*. Milwaukee, WI: Milwaukee Public Museum, Publication in Anthropology no. 6.

Niles, Bertram. 2006. "Are Guyanese Welcome in Barbados?" *BBC Caribbean*, September 7. www.bbc.co.uk/caribbean/news/story/2006/09/060906_guyaneseinbdos.shtml.

Northrup, David. 2000. "Les immigrants indiens engagés aux Antilles françaises (Indentured Indians in the French Antilles)." *Revue Française d'histoire d'outre-mer* 87: 245–71.

Orozco, Manuel. 2002. "Remitting Back Home and Supporting the Homeland: The Guyanese Community in the US." Inter-American Dialogue working paper commissioned by the US Agency for International Development. GEO Project, October 25.

Pancham, Ananta. 2010. "India Association Extols Cultural Pride, Community Service." *St. Thomas Source*, September 4.

Peach, Ceri. 1968. *West Indian Migration to Britain: A Social Geography*. London: Oxford University Press.

Persad, Kamal, and Ashram Maharaj, eds. 1993. "Introduction: H. P. Singh and Indian Nationalism in Trinidad & Tobago" In *The Indian Struggle for Justice and Equality against Black Racism in Trinidad & Tobago (1956–1962)*, by H. P. Singh, xi–lxvii. Chaguanas, Trinidad: Indian Review Press.

Potter, Lesley. 1975. "The Post-Indenture Experience of East Indians in Guyana, 1873–1921." In "East Indians in the Caribbean: Colonialism and the Struggle for Identity," 1–92. Paper presented to a symposium on East Indians in the Caribbean, The University of the West Indies, June.

Prashad, Diane. 2015. E-mail interview with author. London, November 11.

Premdas, Ralph. 1995. "Ethnic Identity in the Caribbean: Decentering a Myth." Lectures and Papers on Ethnicity, no. 17, Robert Harney Program in Ethnic Immigration and Plural Studies. Paper presented at the University of Toronto, Ontario.

———. 2004. "Diaspora and Its Discontents: A Caribbean Fragment in Toronto in Quest of Cultural Recognition and Political Empowerment." *Ethnic and Racial Studies* 27 (4): 544–54.

Puri, Shalini. 2004. *The Caribbean Postcolonial: Social Equality, Post-nationalism, and Cultural Hybridity*. New York: Palgrave Macmillan.

Ramdin, Ron. 2000. *Arising from Bondage: A History of Indo-Caribbean People*. New York: New York University Press.

Ramesar, Marianne. 1994. *Survivors of Another Crossing: A History of East Indians in Trinidad, 1880–1946.* St Augustine, Trinidad: University of West Indies Press.

Ramsoedh, Hans. 2015. E-mail interview with author. The Netherlands, April 8.

Rauf, Mohammed A. 1974. *Indian Village in Guyana.* Leiden: Brill.

Report on Emigration from the Port of Calcutta to British and Foreign Colonies, 1900, Protector of Emigrants. 1901. Calcutta: Bengal Secretariat Press.

Report on Emigration from the Port of Calcutta to British and Foreign Colonies, 1901, Protector of Emigrants. 1902. Calcutta: Bengal Secretariat Press

Report on Emigration from the Port of Calcutta to British and Foreign Colonies, 1904, Protector of Emigrants. 1905. Calcutta: Bengal Secretariat Press.

Report on Emigration from the Port of Calcutta to British and Foreign Colonies, 1906, Protector of Emigrants. 1907. Calcutta: Bengal Secretariat Press.

Report on Emigration from the Port of Calcutta to British and Foreign Colonies, 1911, Protector of Emigrants. 1912. Calcutta: Bengal Secretariat Press.

Rodney, Walter. 1977. "Barbadian Immigration into British Guiana, 1863–1924." Presentation at the Ninth Annual Conference of Caribbean Historians, April, The University of the West Indies, Cave Hill, Barbados.

Roopnarine, Lomarsh. 2001. "Indo-Guyanese Migration: From Plantation to Metropolis." *Immigrants and Minorities* 20 (2): 1–25.

———. 2003. "Indo-Caribbean Migration: From Periphery to Core." *Caribbean Quarterly* 49 (3, Fall): 30–60.

———. 2006. "Return Migration of Indentured East Indians from the Caribbean to India 1838–1920. *Journal of Caribbean History* 40 (2): 308–24.

———. 2007. *Indo-Caribbean Indenture: Resistance and Accommodation.* Kingston, Jamaica: University of the West Indies Press.

———. 2008. "The Other Side of Indo-Caribbean Indentureship: Land-ownership, Savings and Re-migration." *Journal of Caribbean History* 42 (2, December): 205–30.

———. 2009a. "The Repatriation, Readjustment, and Second-Term Migration of Ex-indentured Indian Laborers from British Guiana and Trinidad to India 1838–1955." *New West Indian Guide* 83 (1–2): 71–97.

———. 2009b. "Indian Social Identity in Guyana, Trinidad and North American Diaspora." *Wadabagei: A Journal of the Caribbean and its Diaspora* 12 (3): 87–125.

———. 2010. "The Indian Sea Voyage between India and the Caribbean during the Second Half of the Nineteenth Century." *Journal of Caribbean History* 44 (1): 48–74.

———. 2011. "Indian Migration During Indentured Servitude in British Guiana and Trinidad, 1850–1920." *Labor History* 52 (2): 173–92.

———. 2013. *Guyana Population Movement and Societal Development.* Special Series Working Paper No. 7/12 to commemorate the Fiftieth Anniversary (1963–2013) of the University of Guyana. Institute of Development Studies, University of Guyana.

———. 2014a. "A Critique of East Indian Indentured Historiography in the Caribbean." *Labor History* 55 (3): 389–401.

———. 2014b. "Lecture on 150th Anniversary of the Arrival of East Indians in Danish St. Croix." Paper presented to the Landmark Society of St. Croix, US Virgin Islands, March 10.

———. 2016. "Coolitude: Twenty-five Years Later: Personal Interview with Khan Torabully." *Caribbean Writer* 30: 284–94.

Samaroo, Brinsley. 1975. "Missionary Methods and Local Responses: The Canadian Presbyterians and the East Indians in the Caribbean." In "East Indians in the Caribbean: Colonialism and the Struggle for Identity," 93–116. Paper presented to a symposium on East Indians in the Caribbean, The University of the West Indies, Kingston, Jamaica, June.

———. 1982. "In Sick Longing for the Further Shore: Return Migration by Caribbean East Indians during the Nineteenth and Twentieth Centuries." In *Return Migration and Remittances: Developing a Caribbean Perspective*, edited by W. F. Stinner, K. D. Albuquerque, and R. S. Bryce-Laporte, 45–72. Washington D.C.: Research Institute on Immigration and Ethnic Studies Smithsonian Institution, Riies Occasional Papers, no. 3.

Sannyasi, Bhawani D., and Benardsidas Chaturvedi. 1931. *A Report on the Emigrants Repatriated to India under the Assisted Emigration Scheme from South Africa and on the Problems of Return Emigrants from All Colonies.* Calcutta: Prabasi Press.

Sarusky, Jaime. 1989. "The East Indian Community in Cuba." In *Indenture and Exile: The Indo-Caribbean Experience*, edited by Frank Birbalsingh, 73–78. Toronto: Tsar.

Scoble, John. 1840. *Hill Coolies: A Brief Exposure of the Deplorable Conditions of the Hill Coolies in British Guiana and Mauritius.* London: Harvey & Danton.

Scott, C. James. 1985. *Weapons of the Weak: Everyday Forms of Peasant Resistance.* New Haven, CT: Yale University Press.

———. 1990. *Domination and the Arts of Resistance: Hidden Transcript.* New Haven, CT: Yale University Press.

Segal, Daniel. 1993. "Race and Color in Pre-Independence Trinidad and Tobago." In *Trinidad Ethnicity*, edited by Kevin Yelvington, 81–115. Knoxville: University of Tennessee Press.

Selvon, Sam. 1956. *Lonely Londoners.* New York: St. Martin's Press.

Shepherd, Verene. 1985. "Transient to Citizens: The Development of a Settled East Indian Community." *Jamaica Journal* 18: 17–26.

———. 1986. "From Rural Plantations to Urban Slums: The Economic Status and Problems of East Indians in Kingston, Jamaica, in the late Nineteenth and early Twentieth Centuries." *Immigrants and Minorities* 5 (2): 130–42.

———. 1994. *Transient to Settlers: The Experience of Indians in Jamaica 1845–1950.* Leeds, UK: Peepal Tree Press.

———. 1998. "Indians, Jamaica and the Emergence of a Modern Migration Culture." In *Caribbean Migration: Global Identities*, edited by Mary Chamberlain, 165–76. London: Routledge.

Singh, Chaitram. 1988. *Guyana: Politics in a Plantation Society.* Boulder, CO: Praeger Publishers.

Singh, Rajkumari. 1996. "I am a Coolie." In *The Routledge Reader in Caribbean Literature*, edited by Alison Donnell and Lawson Welsh, 351–53, London: Routledge.

Smith, M. G. 1965. *The Plural Society in the West Indies*. Berkeley: University of California Press.

Smith, Raymond. 1962. *British Guiana*. London: Oxford University Press.

Speckmann, Johan. 1965. *Marriage and Kinship among Indians in Suriname*. Assen, Neth.: Van Gorcum.

Spivak, G. C. 1988. "Can the Subaltern Speak?" In *Marxism and Interpretation of Culture*, edited by Cary Nelson and Larry Grossberg, 271–313. Hemel Hempstead, UK: Harvester Wheatsheaf.

Stoddard, Eve, and Grant Cornwell. 2001. "Miscegenation as a Metaphor for Nation-Building: The 'Douglarization' Controversy in Trinidad and Tobago." In *Global Multiculturalism: Comparative Perspective on Ethnicity, Race and Nation*, edited by Grant Cornwell and Eve Stoddard, 31–55. Lanham, MD: Rowan and Little Field.

Theroux, Paul. 2015. *Deep South*. New York: Houghton Mifflin Harcourt.

Tinker, Hugh. 1974. "A New System of Slavery: Export of Indian Labour Overseas, 1830–1920." London: Oxford University Press.

Tyson, J. D. 1939. *Report on the Conditions of Indians in Jamaica, British Guiana, and Trinidad*. Memorandum of evidence for the Royal Commission to the West Indies presented on behalf of the government of India, New Delhi, India.

"US Immigration Policy and the National Interest." 1981. Committees on the Judiciary House of Representatives and the United States Senate Ninety-Seventh Congress. Washington, DC: U.S Government Printing Office.

Van der Veer, T., and Steven Vertovec. 1991. "Brahmanism Abroad: On Caribbean Hinduism as an Ethnic Religion." *Ethnology* 30 (2): 149–65.

Vertovec, Steven. 1992. *Hindu Trinidad: Religion, Ethnicity and Socio-Economic Change*. London: Macmillan.

———. 2000. *The Hindu Diaspora: Comparative Patterns*. New York: Routledge.

Wallerstein, Immanuel. 1974. *The Modern World-System, Capitalist Agriculture and the Origins of the European World-Economy in the Sixteenth Century*. New York: Academic Press.

Wood, Charles H. 1982. "Equilibrium and Historical-Structural Perspective on Migration." *International Migration Review* 16 (2): 298–319.

Wood, Donald. 1968. *Trinidad in Transition*. London: Oxford University Press.

World Migration Report, International Organization for Migration and the United Nations. 2000. Geneva, Switzerland: The United Nations Migration Agency. www.iom.int/world-migration-report-2000.

INDEX

North American Indian community, 10
North Americanization, 101
nostalgia for India, 139

oil industry, 84
Ontario Society for Services to the Indo-
 Caribbean Community (OSSICC), 137
ordinances, 39–41
Organization of Islamic Cooperation, 140

Pagla Samoondar, 13
paradoxical experience, 142
Paramaribo, Suriname, 48, 73, 94
passports, 52
paupers, 58–59
peasants, 21, 51
People of Indian Origin (PIO), 5
Persad, Diane, 89
pillarization, 94
plantation-derived Hindi, 16
Plantation Port Mourant, 62
Plantation Skeldon, 51
planter class, 46, 55–56
Port Blair, 26
postemancipation Caribbean, 55, 125;
 emigration, 23
postindenture experience, 14–17, 73, 123
postindependence Creole, 75
Pravasi Bharatiya Divas, 139
preexisting values, 7
Premdas, Ralph, 102, 136, 138
Puri, S., 8
push-pull model of migration, 20

Qaseeda competition, 137

racial slur, 131
Ramsoedh, Hans, 52
readjustment, 65–70
recruiters, 24
recruitment, 29–33; false pretenses, 44;
 license, 32
re-indenture, 55, 65
remigration, 65–70
remittances, 16, 54–55, 59–64, 81, 106–7

repatriation, 77
research, 11
returnees, 56–58, 62, 63, 65, 68–69
return migration, 54, 58, 105–6
return passage, 13, 17, 45, 55–56, 58–59
return sea voyage, 63–65
rice and banana industries, 76
rural-urban migration, 17, 21, 45–50
ryotwari, 25

sacrifices, 100, 102
SAFCO, 110
Samaroo, Brinsley, 13, 53, 112, 131
Sanderson Commission, 31
Santan Dharma, 74, 137
Sarnami language, 135
Schenectady, New York, 103–4
Scoble, John, 23
Scott, James, 40
sea voyage, 13, 36–38, 41; return, 63–65
second-born generation, 92
second-generation Caribbean Indians, 100
second-term immigrants, 54, 69
segregation, 50
Shree Ram Naya Sabha Hindu Temple,
 85, 114
Sindhis, 113, 118
Singh, Rajkumari, 129
sirdars, 37
small-scale farmers, 53
social problems, 102
social structure, 65–66, 74, 101
societal orientation classes, 94
South Indians, 15
Speckman, Johan, 49
Spivak, Gayatri, 40
Sriram, 31
standard languages, 7, 124
step migration, 48
structural conditions, 7–8
subaltern, 40
subculture, 100, 142
subservient roles, 133
subworld, 102
suicide, 16, 37, 96, 132

Made in United States
North Haven, CT
18 December 2023

45990872R00107